DISABILITYLAND

DISABILITYLAND

ALAN BRIGHTMAN

FOREWORD BY RICHARD ELLENSON

SELECT BOOKS, INC.

NEW YORK

This edition published by SelectBooks, Inc. For information address SelectBooks, Inc., New York, N.Y. 10003.

DisabilityLand is a revised edition of *Connections: In the Land of Disability* published by Palo Alto Press in 2006.

ISBN 978-1-59079-124-0

Cataloging-in-Publication Data

Brightman, Alan.
 DisabilityLand / Alan Brightman. -- Rev. ed.
     p. cm.
  Rev. ed. of: Connections / Alan Brightman. c2006.
  ISBN 978-1-59079-124-0 (pbk. : alk. paper)
 1. Disabilities. 2. Disabilities--Anecdotes. I. Brightman, Alan.
 Connections. II. Title. III. Title: Disability land.

HV1568.B75 2008
362.4--dc22
                              2007045852

Manufactured in the United States of America

10 9 8 7 6 5 4 3 2 1

Special thanks to the artists and staff of NIAD (National Institute of Art and Disabilities), whose works decorate the pages of this book.

Art Photography by Andrew Nelson

For Melissa. For Alex. For Jesse.
With love. And love. And love.

ACKNOWLEDGMENTS

To so many of my colleagues at Yahoo!, I owe an appreciation that's hard to express. I'm especially grateful to Srinija Srinivasan, Anne Toth, and Ash Patel for helping me better understand the power and the intimacy of the Internet. And to VIctor Tsaran, thanks for letting me see the world through your incredible mind.

From its earliest days, Apple Computer believed that the "Power To Be Your Best" belonged to every individual, disabled and non-disabled alike. I want to thank John Couch, Kathi Fox and Dianna Williamson for keeping that passionate conviction very much alive. Their encouragement and support made this book possible.

All my friends and colleagues at Apple have always made me look a lot better than I ever was. For this I am especially indebted to Peter Green and Gary Moulton. If you care about making good and important things happen in the world, you should know them.

I am grateful also to Robin Coles, Sybil Ellery, Jane Lee, Pam Scutt, Mark Kleid and Peter Lycurgus for the key roles each played in building an organization that touched so many lives.

To Teri Christ and Cindy Kinder, a very special thank you. You mattered more than you know.

Sincere thanks also to Richard Ellenson, whose huge heart and great humor are sprinkled throughout these pages.

To Kris Hill and Richard Wanderman, thank you so much. You enhanced this book the moment you agreed to review early and incomplete drafts.

Susan Thomas turned my writing into pages and then artfully turned those pages into a book. Without her skills, you could be watching TV right now. John Seminerio designed the book and because of him, the pages flow. To each, my heartfelt thanks. By incorporating imagery from NIAD's artists, Janice Benight made a unique contribution to this new version for which I'm so grateful.

Finally, my deepest gratitude to the people who populate the pages of this book. I hope I did justice to what you told me, what you showed me and what you taught me.

With people like these in my life, it's hard to fail. But where I did, it's only because they went out for coffee and left me alone.

✖ ✖ ✖

"THE REAL **VOYAGE** OF

NEW LANDSCAPES BUT IN HAVING

MARCEL PROUST

DISCOVERY CONSISTS NOT IN SEEKING

NEW EYES."

by *Richard Ellenson*

For a few minutes during my son's birth, his body stopped getting oxygen. What was supposed to be a routine birth turned into something quite different. Tom barely made it out of the womb through an emergency cesarean section. Instead of the billing, cooing and nuzzling one envisions after a birth, my memories swirl with bright lights, glaring metal, harshly whispered voices and the tense, worried faces of the Operating Room staff.

Tom spent nearly two weeks in the Neonatal Intensive Care Unit before we took him home. And it was another nine months of missed milestones and slightly off-kilter movements before we found out that the lack of oxygen had created something called basal ganglia involvement; the parts of Tom's brain orchestrating fine motor skills and gross motor skills had died from lack of oxygen. Tom had cerebral palsy.

The journey of our experience is a long one. As one might expect, it contains moments of sadness. But perhaps unexpectedly it contains far more moments of joy. Moments of profound appreciation of another individual, moments of wonder at how many other ways a person can accomplish things and, naturally, moments of what I can only call that gentle thunder of love.

Our son Thomas can't speak and he needs a wheelchair. I expect those two facts to remain that way. But other parts of his brain are fine. The part that holds intelligence, the part that allows receptive language and, certainly, the part that allows an individual to communicate that most elusive of traits: charm.

On top of that, Tom emerged from the firestorm of desperation that surely blazed along his brain's neurons as they felt the chill of dying out with enough determination to still believe in one last lucky tumble of the genetic dice. Tom is a cute kid. Everyone falls for him.

At least that's true now, while he's 8 years old. The wheelchair. The inability to speak. The drool that falls from his mouth and pools up on his shirts. The abnormal movements that sometimes flail about him. None of it matters.

Even when kids don't know quite how to connect with Tom, they are happy to enter that magical space that here, in this book, is so well coined: DisabilityLand. It is as if anyone under the age of 8 breathes some special air that allows him or her to feel natural in Tom's world. They naturally chant the mantras that allow one to navigate this vast and special place, and they embrace its wonders.

However, that isn't always so with adults. People watch Tom and me as we go down the street. We get looks that one can only call sympathy or, at best, empathy. We are, as this book will tell you, *always looked at*.

But you all know the laws of physics: You can't see something's movements if you're on it. The world is spinning at 1,000 miles per hour, but you're sitting on the beach, watching the waves roll forever in front of you.

I have walked beside Tom so attentively now for so long that for me, all else vanishes. We go down streets together, Tom in his wheelchair and me walking beside, and we check out the neighborhood. If it is checking out us, we are unaware of it. We sit over dinner and Tom tells me stories about school or how he wants to be a chef like Emeril or about his latest girlfriend in class; and although this conversation takes places through taps to icons on his wheelchair tray, nods of his head, gazes of his eyes, through low guttural approximations of words—all nuances and milliseconds—that others can't see, for us it is all perfectly natural. It is our life. My heart beats with my son's.

I walk so far into DisabilityLand that I am sometimes taken aback when I journey out.

Our family has worked with the New York City Department of Education to try to improve schools for Tom and so many other amazing kids. As a result, Tom has gotten a fair bit of media exposure. And each time I see my son on TV, I am startled. I want to holler to my wife, Lora, "Look! Look at those abnormal movements. My God! Did you know there might be something wrong with our kid?" It shocks me. When I am in DisabilityLand, I just can't see it.

Lora is a doctor and scientist. She is trained to observe. She understood early on, well before I did, what would be the dance of Tom's life. But I spent my career in advertising. I saw only what the *brand* of disabilities stood for. And, to date at least, that brand stands for unrealized potential and limited ability.

That didn't work for me. For living with Tom, I had been to an amazing place—a place I didn't know existed until I read this wonderful book. Clinging to my hopes and dreams for my magnificent, charming, optimistic and glorious son, he had dragged me right along with him into something even more profound: his reality. An amazing place right at the center of DisabilityLand.

And in the marvelous place about which Alan Brightman writes with such compelling insight, I quickly began to learn and embrace much of what had been out of reach for me.

I am dazzled by the abundance of images and events one finds throughout this book. And, perhaps even more so, by the clearly voracious humanity that has experienced, remembered and shared them all. Alan asks:

"Are people with disabilities that different from any of the other nondescript folks wandering around just like you who you pay no attention to at all?

"In fact, yes. They're different from you and me.

"But you're not supposed to say that in The Land of Disability, where the prevailing motto is 'They're just like everyone else.' So be safe. Stick to the dictum.

"Unless you really, truly, meaningfully want to get to know a few people. And learn how terrifically different they really are."

How could one not be amazed by the twist of logic that leads one to reexamine not just disability but, of course, life itself?

For that is surely what this book is all about. We are all residents of DisabilityLand. If we cannot feel comfortable with the differences of others when they are extreme, how can we feel comfortable with the differences when they are subtler?

Life is about difference. It is about being one of six and a half billion people. About understanding the near infinity of what is possible to do and feel, about experiencing the soaring spirals within which we all come together and then separate again into our own arcs.

Think of it. You are one in six and a half billion. And yet we have the persistent need to feel the acute sense of what it is to be ourselves: an individual. Is it any wonder that so few of us feel truly comfortable within our own skin? Is it any wonder that the journey of life is so daunting until we make the effort to look, with truth and determined honesty, outside of ourselves?

There is no place I would choose to live except in this Land. And to share it with my son, my wife and my daughter. What good fortune to find we have built our home so near one of this Land's great wizards, who has charted this Land so well in the following pages.

New York City
September, 2007

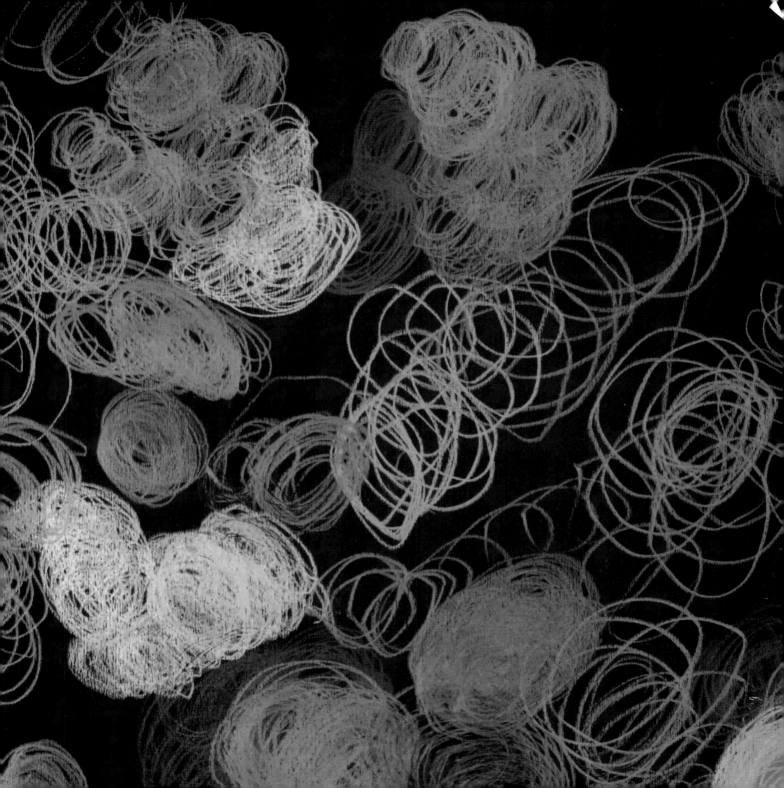

"I re-equip lives. One person at a time.
 Sometimes pieces of a life break. People break.
 They need repairing. That's what I do. I get
 people to say, like they did before they broke,
 'I can do it myself.'"

This is how an occupational therapist described her job. Lives that aren't working quite as they should, she told me, need to be mended.

One life, perhaps, was born without everything it needed. Or some of its parts weren't working correctly. Another life might have flown by too quickly and crumpled in the passenger seat of a car that would never be a car again. Another life may have had a stroke. ("Hadn't been sick a day in my life," said the 42-year-old woman.) And still another reached its 90th year and, like almost anything that age, required at least some retooling to keep running as smoothly as possible.

"I keep lives at the ready," my occupational therapist friend said. "I keep lives living."

This is a book rooted in lives that most of you will never live. Or even come to know. These are lives lived in DisabilityLand.

And where exactly is this Land? Essentially it's anywhere kids and adults with disabilities (together with their families, friends and helpers) run, roll, skip, straggle, try, fall, dream, learn, hope, sing, whisper and succeed. Or not. DisabilityLand is the personal space around anyone with a disability. Maybe in a kitchen. Or a bowling alley. Or a boat. Maybe in a school. Or a hospital. Or, perhaps, a memory.

Not much happens in The Land of Disability that doesn't happen elsewhere. But so much of what goes on there seems to happen in bold relief. When people—disabled and non-disabled people—find themselves in The Land of Disability, they often start acting in italics.

So this is specifically not a book about a word—"disability"—but about a place. In that place, big and little lives play out daily and, sometimes, lessons follow. Many of the lessons are ones that could only have been revealed in The Land of Disability. These are what I've tried to capture and convey.

In some cases, to some readers, some lessons will seem obvious. These you should pass on to others.

✳ ✳ ✳

I have worked in the technology industry—specifically at Apple and at Yahoo!—for more than 2 decades. Before that, I worked in the non-profit sector for 15 years.[1] During all that time, my singular focus was on children and adults with disabilities. Knowing them. Hoping to help them. Being helped by them.

Each of the stories, the questions, and the observations in this book are rooted in those years.

I point this out simply to say that while some of what you'll read in these pages makes specific reference to Apple or Yahoo!, in fact neither company imposed any editorial restrictions or gave me any guidelines other than to be completely candid in what I was writing.

So you'll find some Apple in what follows. And some Yahoo! Both are terrific—and terrifically human—companies with which I'm proud to be associated. But *DisabilityLand* is not about either of these companies. It is instead about people—individuals who in one way or another have spent some time in and around DisabilityLand…

1: All of this, upon reflection, surprises me. I thought I was younger.

...INCLUDING **ME.**

part 1

COMMON NONSENSE

"THERE IS NOTHING WORSE
THAN AGGRESSIVE
STUPIDITY."

JOHANN WOLFGANG VON GOETHE

In one of the wards of the large state school, an attendant noticed that some of the severely retarded young adults had been chewing on the rugs and causing a bothersome amount of damage. What apparently wasn't noticed was the fact that this large, colorless day room, occupied for endless hours by an unchanging collection of semi-clothed individuals, had no books or games or other diversions. There was no opportunity for any kind of stimulation. Rug-chewing was it. The problem could have been easily solved. Bring in some amusements. Some educational materials. Let there be something to do. Let there be life.

That would have been the easy solution. The common sense solution.

The institution's solution was different. The institution's solution was to bring each and every one of the young adults to the institutional dentist to have all of his or her teeth removed. The rug-chewing problem was solved.

Then there was the other problem, a slightly more delicate matter. It seemed that some of the residents were discovering their sexuality. And they were using the trees and bushes of the well-tended grounds to find the only privacy available to them. This set off an institutional alarm. Something needed to be done. But what? Was it right for retarded young adults to know about sex? Was it right for them to experience it? Where does the responsibility lie?

These are not small questions. They linger, largely unanswered, even today. But back then, the institution's first attempt at a suitable response was straightforward: They tore out the offending shrubbery. The only aspect of the institution that was truly beautiful—and truly cared for—was literally uprooted. It was as if the institution's response was, quite simply, "If you want to discover yourself in this way, fine. We don't quite know what to do about it. But you sure won't be doing any discovering behind our bushes."

In a similar institution, the problem was an increase in the number of pregnancies among mildly retarded women who, as a reward for appropriate behavior, were allowed off the grounds on day passes. It seems that some of the local men—the "townies"—were taking easy advantage of these vulnerable women. The institutional response was to implement a new policy whereby the women could no longer go into town on their own. Instead, they had to be paired with a buddy, another woman who had also earned the right to leave the grounds for a day.

Problem solved, the institution believed.

But not exactly.

Within four months, the pregnancy rate doubled.

* * *

Back in the late '60s, a good friend of mine lost a leg in a freak boating accident. A year and a half later, he was called to report to the draft board and, good citizen that he was, he went. With his right pant leg pinned up, he presented himself to the orientation interviewer and sat while she took down his name, address and other demographic information.

Midway through her note taking, the interviewer paused and appeared to be studying her clipboard. She then looked at where his leg used to be and asked, "Will this disability be of lasting duration?"

My friend, the good citizen, said nothing.

He stood up.

And hopped away.

✳ ✳ ✳

Jimmy was 6 years old and deaf. His parents bought him a puppy. Three days later, the parents discovered that the puppy, too, was deaf. They returned the puppy.

He sat on the middle swing all by himself, not moving. Just staring downward, occasionally banging a rhythm on his left leg. Waiting for a push? Waiting for friends?

His overalls were faded, the sleeves of his flannel shirt were frayed and one of his sneakers had fallen to the dirt. They called him Billy. He was 63 years old. They would soon bring him back to class to continue teaching him to write his name in script. Maybe they would succeed where the five previous decades of teachers had failed.

Everything about this scene was wrong to me. Why was this disheveled, overweight man left sitting on a swing meant for young children? Why was he alone and so unkempt? Why did his teachers, at least 40 years his junior, call him Billy?[1] And was there any point at all in

1: Let's say his last name was "Smith." As I watched him sitting on the swing, I wondered if he was *ever in his life* accorded the respect of being called "Mr. Smith."

teaching him—at his age, in this place—to write his name in script?

He was developmentally disabled and had lived in this state school all his life. He'd most likely die here. The only thing certain about his remaining years was that he'd never, ever, *ever* have an occasion where he'd need to write his name at all. Ever.

Never mind writing his name in script.

Many people do today what they did yesterday simply because that's what they did yesterday. Yesterday, they reason, was more or less ok. They act automatically. Unthinkingly.

They press on, trying to teach a 63-year-old man how to wield a crayon.

JUST ASKING.

Think of it, for a moment, this way. If the personal computer had been invented by someone paralyzed from the neck down, do you suppose it would have included a keyboard or a mouse as standard equipment? Or if the personal computer had been invented by someone who was blind, wouldn't it follow that the standard computer screen might have been available only as a special option for sighted users?

But the personal computer wasn't invented by people with disabilities. It was invented instead by some talented engineers who, like most people, had little or no personal experience with disabled others. As a result, obstacles were unintentionally part of the original design.

In most cases the obstacles weren't very big. But then again, the 2-inch curb on the sidewalk doesn't seem to be much of an impediment either.

Unless you're driving a heavy wheelchair.

Years ago I published a book for young children. In it were color pictures of kids I'd come to know over a number of years, each of whom was diagnosed as retarded.

Out of the hundred or so photos, only a few included children with Down syndrome.

"How come you didn't include more pictures of kids who really look retarded?" the adults asked. "How come all but a few look pretty much normal?"

Understand that most of the children in the book had thick files attesting to their various developmental disabilities. These were all, if you will, bona fide retarded kids. But each one's photo reflected a moment in time no longer than 1/60th of a second. And in that instant, the faces that were captured were simply children's faces. Most charming. Most adorable.

Had these same adults seen, say, five minutes of videotape of the kids—their behaviors rather than just their faces—they'd have no question about the kids' problems.

But to them, the faces in the book didn't look like what they imagined the faces of retarded children to be.

Funny, I thought, that when an image of someone doesn't match the prevailing misconception, it must be the picture that's wrong.

✕ ✕ ✕

For the past five years, it seems to me that every conference I've attended on "Education Reform" has been exactly the same.

There's something not right about that.

If the conferences don't change, what chance does Education *Reform* have?

I'm reminded of the teenagers who gather together to assert the importance of their individuality.

"Be yourself."

"Be who you are."

But even amid their odes to uniqueness, most of the teens are dressed almost exactly alike.

"YOU WILL ALWAYS FIND SOME ESKIMOS **READY** TO INSTRUCT THE CONGOLESE ON HOW TO COPE WITH HEAT WAVES."

STANISLAW LEC

"This is a wise woman," my hosts told me. "A very savvy mother."

I shook her tiny hand. To me, more than anything else, she looked sad.

Several years ago, her son was born with one hand slightly disfigured. She demanded that it be amputated immediately.

She had lived all her life in this underdeveloped place and was certain that her son was destined to be a beggar. In her wisdom, she knew that a slight deformity wouldn't generate much sympathy. Or much giving. Without his hand, she reasoned, his begging would be much more effective.

Maybe today that boy is a poet or a programmer or a teacher. But I don't think so. I fear he's a beggar—no doubt a successful one.

✳ ✳ ✳

Onstage in front of hundreds of children who had gathered from around the country to celebrate exceptional young artists with disabilities, the blind celebrity recalled how he'd always been encouraged to pursue his dreams. His rhetoric was stirring. The crowd of children, themselves disabled, applauded throughout, especially when he came to his conclusion:

> "So don't let anyone tell you what you can't
> be. Because you can be anything you want.
> Anything. If you want to be a teacher, be a
> teacher. If you want to be a doctor, be a
> doctor. And if you want to be an astronaut,
> then get going and become an astronaut. And
> don't let anyone or anything get in your way."

He thanked the admiring crowd and walked off the stage waving and smiling. He knew he had done a good job.

What he didn't know and never will, is that at least 14 blind middle-school students felt completely betrayed. "We liked listening to him," one of the girls said later. "We thought he was smart. And we thought he was funny."

"But then," said one of the boys, "he lied to us.

"Who does he think we are? We're blind just like him. And if we know anything, we know—and so should he—that we'll never be able to become astronauts."

"But don't you think that he just said it to get you thinking about your own dreams?"

"But that's the point," said the boy. "He said it. If he didn't mean it, he shouldn't have said it. He shouldn't have reminded us of what we know we'll never be."

✳ ✳ ✳

The Commission had funded a study to see whether an underground subway station needed to be made accessible. The researcher descended two steep flights of stairs to the subway platform and, with his clipboard at the ready, he began observing. And counting.

He did this every day for two weeks.

When the final report was released a month later, the Commission was told that there was no reason to be concerned about the expense of accessibility renovations. In fact, the researcher reported, throughout the entire two-week period only one individual in a wheelchair had used the platform.

"And I don't think it was really a problem for him," noted the researcher. "His friends seemed content to carry him down."

✼ ✼ ✼

"NO ONE TESTS

THE DEPTH OF A RIVER WITH

BOTH FEET."

AFRICAN PROVERB

I was greeted at the entrance to Ward 3 by a smiling, middle-aged woman loosely wrapped in a bright, white lab coat. From one pocket hung a pen fastened with colored ribbon; from another, a ball of keys on a plastic chain. Her costume gave her the look of a surgeon or someone who works in a deli or a janitor. She was, in fact, the Associate Psychologist in this place for men and women with disabilities. She was to be my guide into the world of volunteering.

I was ready. I was anxious. Mostly I was naive. I wanted to be a terrific volunteer. I wanted to help people.

"Why don't you read these files," she suggested, "in order to get to know the patients?"

I was new here. No experience. Certainly no authority. So I didn't question the inverted logic. I just read.

I read about presenting problems and about family backgrounds. I read of fluctuations in test scores and in weight. I read about diagnostic hunches, treatment courses, day-pass privileges and recurring behavioral episodes that certainly seemed, from the writings, to be annoying the staff.

In files whose unnumbered pages averaged more than an inch in thickness, I continued to read others' descriptive phrases, others' numbers, others' assertions, others' questions.

I was getting to know these others pretty well. But I had practically no feel at all for the people they were writing about, the people I could hear behind the locked door in the very next room.

I pretended to finish the reading by late afternoon. I got to know "the patients."

I'd get to know the people tomorrow.

✕ ✕ ✕

"COMMON SENSE IS NOT SO COMMON."

VOLTAIRE

The Cabinet Secretary came to visit Apple. I showed him a 9-minute video of someone with a disability doing something with a computer.

At least once a minute the Secretary chimed, "That's amazing!"

When the tape ended and the final "Amazing" had sounded, I said:

"With respect, sir. It's only amazing to you because you never see it. But for the people who use computers in this way, it's not amazing. It's just ordinary. It goes on every single day of their lives."

He understood immediately and thanked me graciously for pointing out the difference. Then he added, "But it still is amazing, isn't it?"

✳ ✳ ✳

I'd visited this particular building on campus many times. This was the first time I had seen a handicapped access symbol on the door of the first-floor bathroom. Curious to see whether any new ideas or devices had been incorporated into this now usable-by-everyone space, I went in.

The stalls were wider to accommodate people in wheelchairs. Sinks, soap dispensers, towel dispensers and light switches were lowered for the same reason. Easily grabbed aluminum bars were strategically placed to assist in steadying anyone who might have a weakness of one kind or another.

After a minute or so, I determined that there wasn't anything new to learn from this renovation. Everything looked as it should. Everything could be used by everyone.

And then I noticed that the mirrors, which hung over the now-lowered sinks, were fixed at precisely the same height as they were before the renovation. An oversight? I'm sure it was. It would probably be fixed soon enough. But the image lingered. The only thing in a bathroom that literally reflects you, that shows you yourself, remained out of view for people in wheelchairs.

The message, which I'm sure was unintended, sounded something like, "We know you need to use the facilities, too, so we've now made accessible everything that's functional. The mirrors, of course, are only there for aesthetic purposes, so we figured there'd be no reason to lower them.

"Or do aesthetics matter to you, too?"

I don't think it happened that way at all, but physical spaces do communicate in a language of their own.

* * *

JUST ASKING.

Ask any disabled person what the toughest thing is about being disabled. Know what he or she will tell you?

It's not the pain or the dependence or the expense or even the inaccessible bathroom. The toughest thing about being disabled is that you're never perceived as just plain ordinary. Because when you're disabled, the world always looks at you as someone special, as someone exceptional.

When you're disabled, the world looks at you as someone who doesn't quite fit in.

You'll also be told that society still too often regards disabled folks as a group that the rest of us have to take care of, a group that has very limited options, opportunities or degrees of freedom. They contribute very little because, let's face it, that's the most they can do. And they require an awful lot.

But because we, the non-disabled, understand the specialness of their condition and because we like to think of ourselves as charitable, we agree to take care of them.

Here's what else disabled folks will tell you.

We don't want to be taken care of. Even that patronizing attitude is repulsive to us. In fact, we want to participate as fully and as richly as we can, and we want to contribute no less than anyone else. We want to exercise as many options and choices as we possibly can.

You know why?

Because we can.

We want to laugh often and live our lives out loud.

You know why?

Because we can.

But most of all, we want to dream new dreams. And then we want to realize as many of our dreams as possible.

You know why?

Of course you do.

"PEOPLE STRUGGLE NOT ONLY TO DEFINE THEMSELVES, BUT TO AVOID BEING DEFINED BY OTHERS. BUT **TO BE A CRIPPLE** IS TO LEARN THAT NO ONE CAN BE DEFINED FROM OUTSIDE."

LEONARD KRIEGEL

The young blind women in Ghana were being trained to be bakers, and from their open clay ovens they turned out impressive loaves of bread that they had created from scratch. The entrepreneur saw a better way for them, a way that would significantly increase their efficiency. They would be able to make more product, generate more profit, enhance the quality of their lives.

He sold them large ovens, propane driven, metal.

As soon as they began to use the new technology, the blind women failed miserably. Same ingredients. Lousy bread.

Unlike the open clay ovens, the propane versions required doors. Which meant that the bakers' sense of smell—what they relied on to determine when the bread was done—was rendered useless.

If they couldn't smell it, they couldn't bake it.

✕ ✕ ✕

My exhibition of photographs was opening tonight at the John F. Kennedy Library in Boston. The Brahmins would be there in tuxedos. My friends would be there, too. Not in tuxedos. And the guests of honor would be the people in the pictures—50 individuals, young and old, who among them shared roughly a hundred different diagnostic labels.

The exhibit was titled *Ordinary Moments: Expressions of the Disabled Experience,* and the people in the photographs were doing nothing special. They weren't Poster Children. They weren't asking for charity. Nor were they triumphing heroically in the face of overwhelming odds. They were just being themselves, doing the mundane. If there was a message, that was it. Most moments of most disabled people's lives are not moments of melodrama. They're lives. Just as boring and matter-of-fact and joyous and difficult and silly and…as ordinary as any other lives.

I looked forward to the mix of cultures at this evening's opening. The wealthy. The far-from-wealthy. And the labeled. I couldn't imagine that before this evening, these three groups would ever have shared the same physical space. Certainly they wouldn't share the same dress code. Maybe tonight would be a source of inspiration for a follow-up exhibition: *Awkward Moments: A Wheelchair Rolled Over My Gown.*

I also looked forward to creating an environment for the evening that would be a model of accessibility. Everyone would be able to easily do what everyone else was doing. Eating. Drinking. Viewing. Schmoozing. Every aspect of this impressive setting would be usable by all, to be enjoyed by all.

But it didn't turn out that way.

"How could you, of all people, be so thoughtless?" he asked me. I didn't know who he was, never mind what he was talking about. But he was someone from the wealthy crowd. And he had no visible signs of any disability.

"Excuse me?" I said. "What seems to be the problem?"

"Walk with me to the bar," he said.

I did.

"Now what do you see?"

I looked.

"See what I mean?"

I didn't.

"Look at all those bottles," he said, pointing to the cloth-covered table. "All that liquor. Very impressive, I'm sure. But not to me. There's nothing here for me to drink."

He'd said a lot, but I still had no idea why he was upset. There on the bar were all shapes and sizes of glasses and cups and straws and holders, all within easy reach of anyone in a wheelchair. No one else seemed to be having a problem. What was his?

I asked.

And he answered, "I have diabetes. Now do you get it?"

I didn't.

"You've got all kinds of soda on that bar," he continued. "But none of it is sugar-free. So what am I supposed to drink?"

Now I got it. No matter how thoroughly I'd thought about accessibility, the need for sugar-free mixers never entered my mind. And this individual, as a result, was left out. His drinks were inaccessible to him. He was un-included.

I'd learned my lesson. That will never happen again.

But something else will, I'm sure. Something just as embarrassing, just as awkward and just as thoughtless.

The lessons never end.

✳ ✳ ✳

"FOR EVERY EXPERT, THERE IS AN EQUAL AND **OPPOSITE EXPERT.**"

ARTHUR C. CLARKE

He began fifth grade with his fingernails intact and his parents well liked by every teacher he'd ever had. Neither the nails nor his parents' good standing would make it to Thanksgiving.

There's an activity that's familiar to many parents of kids with disabilities. "A strange treasure hunt," one father called it, in which the searching continues until just the right diagnostic label's been discovered…the label that increases the likelihood of additional special services. If the journey ends successfully, then those special services are written into the child's IEP and they become, legally, required.

But good teachers don't need to be guided by requirements. That's why they're called good teachers. They understand that no two children learn alike.

Good teachers adapt lessons to match individual learning styles and, as much as possible, to ensure successful outcomes. In the eyes of good teachers, every child learns and every child succeeds.

Good teachers add inches to every child's self-esteem.

This fifth grader had no diagnostic label and, therefore, no IEP. What he had instead was a history of good teachers and a tutor hired by his parents. And as his struggles with learning (especially reading, spelling and writing) became more apparent with each new grade, each new teacher made the accommodations necessary for him to perform at his grade level.

No legally formalized requirements. Just good teaching.

And then came fifth grade. Accommodating stopped. No child would be singled out for special treatment, the new teacher declared. And, further, no piece of paper required her to do so.

The parents spoke with her and got nowhere. To fully appreciate what "nowhere" means, consider the teacher's explanation: "Your child is performing at his grade level and therefore requires no special treatment."

Well *of course* he's performing at his grade level. But only *because* of the special treatment and tutoring he's been receiving. Take some of that away and guess what happens: more struggling, less succeeding and blown self-confidence.

You know what else happens? Mom and Dad become warriors. Unless they want to stand by while he flails his way to failure, they have no choice but to battle.

Once well liked and respected, suddenly Mom and Dad are the enemy. It's a transformation that too many parents have had to undergo. It's also a very well-kept secret, a quiet byproduct of bad teaching: Good parents, according to the school, can go bad.

And the fingernails. How did they, too, suddenly go bad?

One morning, the teacher made a surprise announcement. *All* of her students—no exceptions, she said—were going to be entered in the upcoming schoolwide spelling bee. "So practice up everyone. There's not much time."

By the next morning, the fifth grader's nails were gone.

Gone bad. Just like his parents.

✳ ✳ ✳

"THIS **ISN'T** RIGHT.

THIS ISN'T EVEN WRONG."

WOLFGANG PAULI

"I used to be just a kid. Now all of a sudden,
I'm a patient. It's like they forgot I'm still really
just a kid. So now they lie to me. 'Don't worry,'
they say with a smile, 'It won't hurt.'

"Then they talk about me behind my back…
right in front of me."

In money and miles, the program dwarfed anything we'd ever done at Apple. It wound around the globe and included thousands of children and families with chronic illnesses or disabilities. It was intimate and loud and energetic. Most importantly, it was unfailingly honest.

We built *Convomania*[3] for seriously ill and often disabled children, young people who were spending too many weeks a year—sometimes months—in the hospital. They had very long diagnostic labels attesting to how much "not good" was happening in their bodies and their lives. And they had parents who, it seemed, were in a constant state of waiting for the next set of test results and whose refrigerator doors were crowded with notes about upcoming appointments with doctors.

Most striking to me, these hospitalized kids began way too many sentences with the words, "I miss…"

3: I can't remember why we called it, strangely, *Convomania*. Maybe it had something to do with the words "conversation" and "convalescence." Probably it had more to do with enabling the kids who participated in the program to refer to themselves as "maniacs."

One missed "going fishing with grandpa." Another missed "playing catch with my brother." Still another missed "spending time with my girlfriend" or "show-and-tell at school."

One girl said she missed "my smile."

Many of them said they missed their hair.

And more than a few realized that they were also missing their own childhood.

Contrary to how hospitalized children are popularly portrayed, these were kids who spent much of their hospital time being, as Reynolds Price describes, "brave as blowtorches."[4] And when they weren't being valiant, they were stunningly bored. During most of their stay, they were kids who simply waited. And who continued to miss.

As one of them said, "It's hard to be sick when you're sick."

Convomania was designed to reconnect these disconnected kids. It grew into a large online community where seriously ill and disabled kids around the world connected at all hours to offer each other support, encouragement and, especially, the truth.

The citizens of *Convomania* made this virtual space "the place to be" for a lot of very sick kids. They showed up from around the world to participate in group

4: *A Whole New Life: An Illness and a Healing,* Scribner, 2003.

forums and individual chats. They discussed how they first learned about their illnesses, how their parents reacted to the diagnoses, what it was like to enter the hospital for the first time (and then for the twenty-first time) and whether close friends back home were still close friends back home. They all knew when one of them was having an unusually tough time, facing a particularly difficult procedure and an uncertain outcome. "We'll be right there with you," was a common response among members who lived states—and sometimes countries—apart.

We knew that the sharing that was happening all over *Convomania* was having an impact when we began hearing from doctors: "I don't want my patients to be getting information from anyone else but me. Understood?"

We did understand. But we didn't entirely agree.

✻ ✻ ✻

We'd been examining all the sites across the Yahoo! network to determine which ones needed improvements in accessibility for disabled web surfers.

Today we were looking closely at the site where cars were bought and sold online. It's called Yahoo! Autos.

The person in charge of the site welcomed our intervention. And when we were done we pointed out how some functions of the site were not accessible to blind people who were using screenreaders to access the Internet.

"I don't mean to sound harsh or uncaring," he said. "But just between you and me, why would a blind person want to be using Yahoo! Autos? I mean, he's blind right?"

He wasn't being harsh or uncaring. He was being honest and innocent.

We gave him six different reasons before he stopped us.[1] "I get it," he said. "I'd just never before thought about a blind person in that way."[2]

✝ ✝ ✝

1: I could list the 6 reasons here, but that would be too easy. If you're curious about why a blind person would want to visit Yahoo!Autos...ask a blind person.
2: Just a guess since I never asked: Apparently "In that way" means "As a well rounded, interested human being."

part II

LEARNINGS

"IT IS NEVER TOO **LATE** TO

BE WHAT YOU MIGHT HAVE BEEN."

GEORGE ELIOT

In 1984, in Cupertino, California, thousands of young men and women became convinced that "a personal computer can change your life." Not merely enhance it. Not just make it more efficient or more productive or more fun. No, these people believed that the personal computer could actually—fundamentally—change your life.

They worked for Apple Computer, a company and a culture where people wore their convictions, quite literally, on their sleeves. And on their chests. And where they stamped their beliefs on ubiquitous bumper stickers and buttons. A few even on the sides of their wheelchairs.

A computer can change your life.

This idea defined Apple's mission and drove Apple employees to work endless hours. Weeks for these people had no weekends. Their other T-shirt read "Working 90 hours a week…and loving it." The lights at Apple were always on. The parking lots, like the bike racks, were always full.

A long-term project was usually due by the end of the week.

A computer can change your life.

This wasn't a passion restricted to the engineering community. Everyone seemed to own it, no matter where in the company they worked. Ask them why they did what they did—no matter what that happened to be—and at some early point in their answer they would talk about changing the world, one person at a time. Because, of course, *a computer can change your life.*

I was a new employee and the enthusiasm swirling about was exhilarating and infectious. It was easy to get swept up. And, easily, I did. After having spent my entire life on the East Coast, working in nonprofit organizations and trying to assist disabled individuals, here I was in the middle of a West Coast revolution having to do with transforming lives.

I was fueled—and in a strange way comforted—by the tirelessness and the intensity all around me. These were attributes, after all, that very much defined the culture of the nonprofit arena as well. This Apple energy felt familiar. Hadn't I, too, been involved in passionate efforts to help people?

But never on this change-your-life scale.

My efforts had been significantly more focused and far less dramatic. I'd worked, for example, with parents whose retarded children needed to learn how to dress and feed themselves, how to communicate, how to develop skills for independent living. I'd worked, too, with the young staffs of state schools and institutions who believed that their disabled charges simply needed "more love, man" if they were ever going to participate meaningfully in society.[7]

Action and achievement counted for a lot in our work. Rhetoric counted for just about nothing. We didn't do slogans. We did solutions. We did deeds. We followed the pragmatic tutoring of Alice Roosevelt Longworth: "Fill what's empty. Empty what's full. And scratch where it itches."

As a result, we didn't extol the virtues of change. We modified the things that needed to be different. We didn't hold out the promise of help. We helped.

Despite my initial enthusiasm, I was growing concerned by the Apple rhetoric. If it were true, I reasoned, that a computer can change your life, then wasn't this more of a comment on your life than on the computer?

A computer can change your life.

If this is so—if this plastic box neatly crammed with wires and silicon chips could actually change your life—then what kind of a life must you have?

I was wholly captivated by Apple. By its people and by its culture. I was, however, growing wary of the rhetoric. I was beginning to doubt that a computer could in fact change a life. Or even that it should.

I would soon be given the opportunity to create something that turned me into a believer. Something that did indeed change lives. Sometimes subtly. Sometimes dramatically. Even a few times magically.

One life, in particular, was changed more than any other.

My own.

47

II

* * *

7: No one argued against the proposition that the residents of the institution needed "more love." The more, the better. We did point out, however, that love, by itself, never toilet trained anyone.

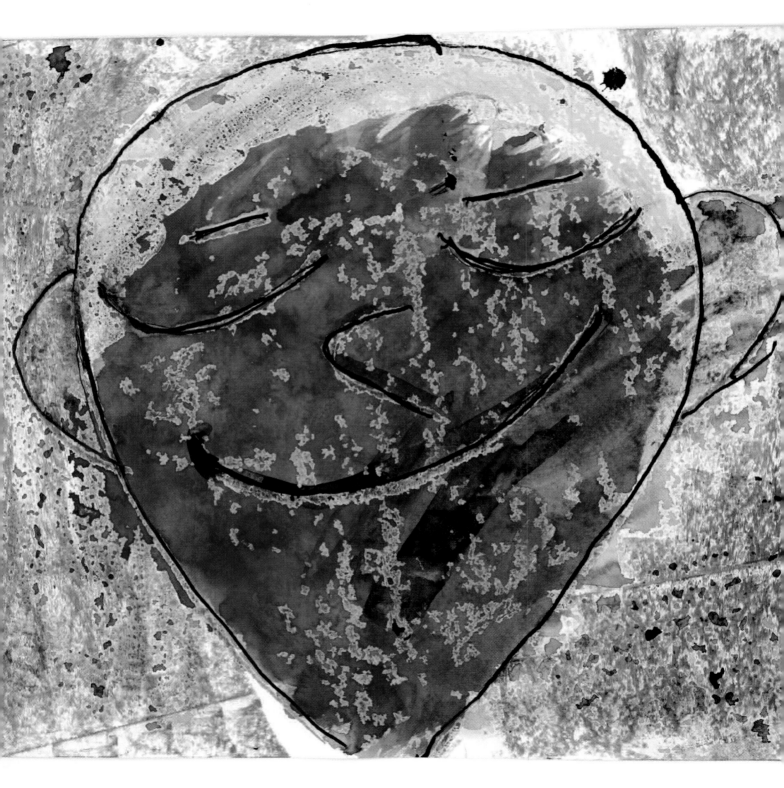

"THE GREAT MAJORITY OF MEN ARE **BUNDLES** OF BEGINNINGS."

RALPH WALDO EMERSON

"How does that kid in the wheelchair go to the bathroom?"

"Why does that blind girl keep her eyes open?"

"If I yell into that deaf kid's ear, will he hear me better?"

You can tell right away that these questions weren't asked by adults. Not because they're simple (they're not), but because they are to the point. From the gut. And not necessarily polite.

These are questions from people who actually want answers. **That's what kids ask.**

Adults, on the other hand, usually don't ask. Instead, they smile. "The child with a disability is just like you and me." And they spout. "A retarded child is a child first; and only then should he or she be seen as retarded."

These kinds of well-intentioned but ill-informed bloviations have two things in common: 1) to a child, they are at best confusing and usually meaningless; and 2) they are safe. In DisabilityLand, adults work hard at feeling comfortable. At pretending not to notice.

The Child asks: "Why does that retarded kid do that stupid stuff?"

The Teacher answers: "Don't you think it's time we finished our spelling lesson?"

When I wheel into a cocktail party, he told me, I can tell right away what all those new faces are seeing. It's how they look at me. Well, not really me. My chair. To them I'm a 6-inch guy in a 10-foot wheelchair.

So yet again—because it matters—I have my work cut out for me. I'll have to put things back in proper proportion for them.

To me, it never doesn't matter.

* * *

"LET ME LISTEN TO ME AND NOT TO THEM."

GERTRUDE STEIN

Anyone who's spent much time in The Land of Disability has been asked, by the tourist, "What word should I use? What should I call them?"

The concern and discomfort reflected in these questions was summarized best by the public relations professional who asked, "Can you teach me how not to sound stupid?"

Debates about "the right word" have always raged in DisabilityLand and there's no sign that the arguments are letting up. But just how important, in fact, is "the right word"?

I finally figured it out. The conference speakers helped me put "the right word" in its proper place.

The conference was focused on the virtues of community-based living for developmentally disabled adults. These were people who had lived for many years in large institutions and who had since been "de-institutionalized" to live, work and play among the rest of us. How could that be anything but idyllic?

But this particular session asked whether there were aspects of life in the community that were *not* so wonderful? What problems, specifically, needed to be addressed?

The panel of experts consisted of five retarded adults, 45 to 55 years old. All of them were having a tough time finding a good job. One problem. Finding good roommates wasn't easy either. Another problem. And then came the problem that related to "the right word."

This is how it was discussed among the experts:

"Why is it that people who have no trouble talking a mile a minute always pause when they need to use a word that describes who we are?"

"How do I call you?" one interviewer had asked. "What word do I use?"

"They should just use my name, right? That's what they should call me, right?"

And then one of the experts stood up, introduced himself as "Charles-not Charlie" and announced the following:

"For all of you so-called experts in the audience, I will now solve the problem. I will tell you the word you should use."

We leaned forward and the room went silent. Charles paused a moment, obviously enjoying the attention, and then said, "From now on, if you bump into any of us on the street and you're looking for a word to describe us, just use the word…"

Another pause.

"…just use the word 'retardate,' ok?"

We in the audience had expected something different, certainly a word that was less clinical, less distant. "Retardate? That's the right word? Couldn't be."

Then, with a sly smile, Charles went on to say, "And when we need to refer to you, we'll just use the word…"

He paused again.

"…we'll use the word 'normate,' ok?"

As far as I was concerned, the debate over "the right word" had just been forever put to bed.

✂ ✂ ✂

From the beginning, the personal computer was about speed and about power.

"You can do more," the ads said.

"You can do more, faster."

"You can do more, faster and better."

In DisabilityLand, however, these weren't the messages that most mattered. For children and adults with disabilities, the message was more humble, more intimate, quiet. What it conveyed, unspoken, was "You can do things." Period.

From "I can't" to "Well, just maybe I can." From "Here's who you are" to "Here's who you might become."

When you're disabled and you have access to a personal computer, you quickly discover that you have access to new parts of yourself. The playing part. The learning part. The working part. The social part. The communicating part.

And, of course, the part that dreams and imagines. And hopes.

You begin to experience yourself in new ways.

And maybe most importantly, you find yourself in a position to do the one thing you've been wanting to do forever: Let the world know who you are. Your definition of yourself. Not anyone else's.

So while the ads shout about speed and power, you know that the computer is about something much more exhilarating.

Identity.

Yours.

✳ ✳ ✳

JUST ASKING.

Are people with disabilities that different from any of the other nondescript folks wandering around just like you who you pay no attention to at all?

In fact, yes. They're different from you and me.

But you're not supposed to say that in DisabilityLand, where the prevailing motto is "They're just like everyone else." So be safe. Stick to the dictum.

Unless you really, truly, meaningfully want to get to know a few people. And learn how terrifically different they really are.

"You should see what you look like when
you're looking at me."

Jamie was 13 years old and a little person. She bristled if she was called a "dwarf."

One afternoon, a boy of about 5 or 6 came up to her and asked how she got to be so small. Normally, this would have been an opportunity for Jamie to do a little teaching, something she enjoyed and something she did "nine million times a week." But on this day, she felt she'd already answered enough questions about her size. She didn't want to teach anymore. So she looked directly at the boy and replied, "One night when I was about your age, my mother was helping me take a bath, and she accidentally left me in the tub too long. So I shrunk."

"Mean, right?" Jamie said to me. "Ok, so I'm not always perfect. But you try answering personal questions from strangers all the time. See if you don't sometimes get a little frustrated.

"By the way, you should have seen the look on that kid's face."

That same year, Jamie was invited to a school dance by a boy who was also a little person. She'd been to many dances before, but never with anyone her own size. The next day, when asked about the event, she answered, "I loved it. And finally I got to know what my friends mean when they say slow dancing is so sexy."

Laura was 14 and, with several of her girlfriends, she was determined to discover "what drinking was all about." Since they already knew an older boy who could get them "some beers," the rest of their plan was simple. They'd first read as many reviews as they could find about a particular movie and then they'd tell their parents they were going to see that film. When asked later about the movie, they'd know what to say.

Laura was blind.

Later that night, when she returned home, Laura's mother was waiting for her in the kitchen. "How was the movie?" she asked. As Laura launched into her prearranged critique, she had no idea that her breath was betraying her. And since her mother just kept listening, Laura just kept talking.

"That's why I was grounded," she'd say later. "Since my mother wasn't saying anything and since I couldn't see her reaction to my story, I had no idea that my lie was failing. I guess that's probably one of the toughest things about being blind," she continued. "I'll just never be able to lie as well as my friends."

✳ ✳ ✳

"DON'T BE AFRAID

TO TAKE A BIG STEP IF ONE IS

INDICATED. YOU CAN'T CROSS

A CHASM IN TWO SMALL JUMPS."

DAVID LLOYD GEORGE

Most corporate meetings are forgettable. This one began that way, too. And then it became indelible.

Around the table were Apple's brightest hardware and software designers credited, many of them, with beginning the personal computer revolution. They had created the Apple II. And then they had created Macintosh. They knew computers.

Also around the table was an invited group of rehabilitation clinicians and rehabilitation engineers from around the country. These were professionals responsible less for revolutions than for evolutions. These were people who designed and built things to help individuals with disabilities. They knew people.

And then there was us, a pair of people from Apple's newly created Office of Special Education.[8] We didn't know much... but we knew enough to assemble everyone else.

After the obligatory round-the-table introductions, some brief presentations and the screening of a videotape ("Check it out," one of the Apple engineers whispered pretty much to himself, "he's actually typing with his toes."), we presented the group with a challenge. That's when the meeting turned memorable.

Till now the group had talked a lot about accessibility, about how some people negotiated their environment differently than others. We talked about obstacles, about curb-cuts, about whether ease of use was always easy. It was good talk. But it was talk. And we knew we needed action.

8: Apple officially announced its new Office of Special Education in 1985 with a press release. If the release had been completely forthcoming, it would have made a slightly different announcement. We didn't actually have an Office when we began. We had a cubicle. We were the "Cubicle of Special Education." But when visitors showed up, we were easy to find. We were a mere 30 yards from the corporate popcorn machine. As this office grew to encompass all individuals with disabilities, it was renamed the Worldwide Disability Solutions Group.

So we sat each engineer in front of a Macintosh, the computer they'd designed, the one they knew more intimately than anyone else. Next to each Macintosh we placed a disk loaded with MacWrite, a simple word processing program. And we said:

> "In front of you is a Macintosh. You know more about this personal computer than anyone else. Also in front of you is MacWrite. You all know how to use it, right?"

Nods all around.

> "Good. Now what we want you each to do is put your hands in your pockets, put a pencil in your mouth and type a simple memo. You can begin any time."

Silence.

The first protest came almost immediately. "Wait a minute. Before I play your game, I'm going to have to turn the thing on, aren't I? It's going to be impossible to reach that On/Off switch if all I can use is a pencil in my mouth." [9]

"Not only that," came the second, "what about when I have to hold down two keys at the same time? How am I supposed to manage that with a pencil? And sometimes I have to hold down three keys..."

9: This particular switch was located on the back of the computer.

"A pencil and a mouse," said the third. "Talk about two things that just don't go together..."

The real meeting had begun and in less than an hour—during which the participants were encouraged to experiment as well with closed fists, earmuffs and blindfolds—Apple's best and brightest discovered that many of the features they'd always considered to be conveniences in the Macintosh could easily be quite the opposite for users less facile than themselves.

One engineer put weights on her typing hand and soon discovered that when she pressed any key, the corresponding letter on her screen kept repeating and repeating and repeating until she was finally able to lift her heavy hand off the keyboard. ("One step forward," she observed, "and a lot of steps backwards.")

"And listen to this," said a different engineer. "When the Macintosh needs to get my attention, it beeps at me, right? Every Macintosh does. Which is a nice convenience, right?" The room nodded. The engineer then slipped on a pair of earmuffs, raised his voice a notch or so, for effect, and challenged the nods: "But what if I were deaf? Then the beep is pretty much irrelevant, isn't it? So, I ask you, how do I get my Macintosh to alert me if I can't hear it?"

The exercise was working. That engineer told us later that he'd never before even thought about deaf people, never mind about their computing needs.

He still works at Apple. And today, he says, he thinks about everyone.

✻ ✻ ✻

From the beginning, we made sure that *Convomania* was at least one place in the world (real or virtual) where hospitalized sick kids would not be regarded only as patients. We were determined to view them as they ought to be viewed. As kids.

In retrospect, our determination was misguided. We'd been trying too hard to be…nice, when in fact, as we were abruptly reminded by a 16-year-old Convomaniac, we should have been more honest with ourselves.

> "We appreciate that you've designed this place where we can do all kinds of things and talk to all kinds of people and break all kinds of rules. We appreciate that you designed a really fun place for kids.
>
> "But now you also have to create a different kind of place. You need to make a place specifically for really sick kids.
>
> "Because we can't forget that that's who we are.
>
> And neither should you."

✳ ✳ ✳

"**LIFE** IS A LONG

LESSON IN HUMILITY."

JAMES M. BARRIE

We counseled parents to be wary of the rhetoric that too often swirls around children with disabilities. Just because someone has a fancy degree, we'd caution, doesn't mean you have to nod in agreement when he's talking about your child. You're as much an expert in this matter as he is and, in many ways, more.

So, we urged, when the jargon gets too thick (or when the professional gets too precious), your job is to ask one simple question: **"What do you mean by that?"** And ask it over and over again until you get an answer you can understand.

> "He's a dandy young boy, Mrs. Smith," said the voice. "Lots of potential. Which is why this year, we at the XYZ School are going to concentrate on strengthening Herbert's ego boundaries."

"What do you mean by that? (And how would I ever be able to know if you've succeeded?)"

"Well, we believe that Herbert's ego boundaries ought to be, you know, stronger," said the voice, with increased conviction.

"And what, may I ask once again, do you mean by that?"

"Well, it's hard for a layman to understand, Mrs. Smith…"

She interrupted. "Then make it simple for me."

He replied, "I'm still not sure you'll comprehend…"

She interrupted again. "And what exactly do you mean by *that*?"

Here are two definitions for the word "handicapped."

The first, on this page, comes from *The American Heritage® Dictionary of the English Language* (Fourth Edition, Houghton Mifflin Company, 2000) and is helpfully accompanied by a "usage note."

The second, on the next page, comes from a friend of mine named Ed, a young adult with muscular dystrophy. Ed didn't append a usage note to his definition. He didn't need to.

> hand·i·capped
> *adj.*
> Physically or mentally disabled:
> *n. (used with a pl. verb)*
> People who have a physical or mental disability
> considered as a group. Often used with *the.*

Usage Note: Although *handicapped* is widely used in both law and everyday speech to refer to people having physical or mental disabilities, those described by the word tend to prefer the expressions *disabled* or *people with disabilities.* Handicapped, a somewhat euphemistic term, may imply a helplessness that is not suggested by the more forthright *disabled.* It is also felt that some stigma may attach to the word *handicapped* because of its origin in the phrase *hand in cap*, actually derived from a game of chance but sometimes mistakenly believed to involve the image of a beggar. The word *handicapped* is best reserved to describe a disabled person who is unable to function owing to some property of the environment. Thus people with a physical disability requiring a wheelchair may or may not be *handicapped,* depending on whether wheelchair ramps are made available to them.

✕ ✕ ✕

Handicapped: A Definition[10]

Being handicapped is when you're the guest of honor at the "Handicapped Person of the Year" award luncheon and the restroom doors are too narrow for the wheelchair so you have to urinate in a broom closet.

Or when someone actually says to you, "Oh, you have muscular dystrophy? If that happened to me, I'd kill myself."

Not being able to turn the radio on. Or the television off.

Accomplishing microscopic tasks well.

Going to the museum and getting in free.

Seeing everything from always only 4 feet off the ground.

Hating having to ask. All the time ask.

Having the ability to sit in one place for nine hours without going mad from restlessness. And after nine hours of not moving, coming home to sit in a different chair for seven hours more.

Being handicapped is worrying about being handicapped too much.

But damn it, this room is a mess and I can't clean it. I'm hungry and I can't cook. The window is open and it's freezing outside; I can't shut it. The record player's skipping but the bike's in the way of the player. I hate that scratching noise.

I can't find a pipe that's not clogged, so I can't even get high.

The incredible pettiness gets wearing at times. I'm always worrying about getting to bed, getting up, getting into a chair, getting out of a chair.

Being handicapped creates a pettiness syndrome. All you think about is simple stuff.

✳ ✳ ✳

10: From A. Brightman, ed., *Ordinary Moments: The Disabled Experience,* University Park Press, 1984.

He sat in his wheelchair among the growing group of demonstrators, listening to anti-war speeches, folk songs and an occasional supportive yelp. Some in the group were his friends. Many he was meeting for the first time. He looked like he was enjoying himself. He looked like he belonged. We talked in the van on the way home.

"Did you have a great time?" I asked.

"Not after about 20 minutes," he answered.

We had stayed more than four hours. "Why?"

"Too many times I caught people staring at me, the only wheelchair in the bunch."

"And?"

"They were looking at me too much."

"Anything else?"

"And many of the folks, even the ones sitting close to us, never looked my way once. Like I was invisible."

"So what's any of this got to do with whether you had a good time?"

"It just annoys me," he said. "It's not cool when I get stared at. It's even less cool when I'm not noticed.

"Welcome to being me."

✻ ✻ ✻

When she was born, they didn't think she'd survive for more than a day. Then a week went by. She was still breathing. Then another week, then a month, then many more months.

She didn't die.

Today she lives in a large, tile-walled institution laying completely still all day long in a crib. She's silent and completely dependent on others for every aspect of her life. She's 22 years old.

She was supposed to die at birth. She's survived for 22 years.

Is that a success or a failure?

✳ ✳ ✳

It's often referred to as the *invisible* disability or the *hidden* disability. But look closely at the face of any student with a learning disability who's struggling with reading or math or spelling. **Look even closer** at the face of any student with a learning disability who's just trying to "pass" in the classroom.

Reflected in these faces are the often pained expressions that show just how visible, in fact, learning disabilities are.

Learning disabilities, when you look, are all too apparent. They may be among the least well-hidden disabilities of all.

When we first announced that Apple was starting a division to focus on the specific needs of disabled children and adults, Apple employees had the following reactions:

"What a nice thing for the company to be doing."

"Think there'll be an Apple poster child?"

"Probably it'll be about philanthropy."

Apple employees, after all, were like most people in the world when it came to knowing people with disabilities. They didn't. And so they reacted in a fairly predictable way. They responded to the stereotypes that surround disability.

We weren't creating a new division because it was nice. We were doing it because it was smart. Apple was a mainstream company making products for a mainstream society, and if those products were designed with disabled users in mind, then it's likely that Apple would sell more computers.

There, of course, wouldn't be any poster children. Apple's initiative was about being savvy not sappy; sincere not symbolic.

Most importantly, the new undertaking would have nothing to do with philanthropy. I have yet to meet any individual with a disability who wanted to be seen as an object of charity. Instead, the new division would regard people with disabilities as demanding and discerning consumers. They would be new customers. Not new causes.

Today they're not new anymore.

* * *

JUST ASKING.

We were often[11] asked by teachers and by parents, "What's the best special education software?" Or, similarly: "My daughter has a learning disability. What software should I get for her?" Or, similarly: "My son was recently placed in a mainstream class. What software should I get for him?" And so on.

It's an important question. I understand why it was asked so much. And, of course, it remains forever unanswerable.

Two reasons.

Software isn't written for a diagnostic label, just as software isn't written for a person's name. You might as well ask for software written for someone who wears a size 9 shoe.

More importantly, there is no such thing as special education software. Really. There's good software and there's not-so-good software. There's software that says "special education" on the packaging and there's software that says nothing about any kind of education at all.

How to decide?

Go for the good software and ignore the packaging. Go with what works best for your unique situation. That'll be your best special education software.

But keep one important point always in mind. It doesn't have to be "educational software" to be educational software. Computer programs that help kids to draw, to play music, to make up silly sounds... none of these are expressly considered "educational." But in the hands of a good teacher, they might be just what the student needs to reach a particular goal.[12]

Then of course there's the Internet, home of more great software for special education than you'll find anywhere else. And it's all free... at least to try.

So let's review. What's the best education software?

Still unanswerable. For me.

But for you, no longer.

11: By "often" I mean more than any other question every year for more than a dozen years.

12: Conversely, great educational products in the hands of a not-very-good teacher will usually not fare well.

"When I think back to grammar school, I remember the special class as a worse place to be threatened with than the principal's office. But I don't remember why. Perhaps I never really knew. Perhaps the mysteries of unexplained difference (I remember that 'they' weren't like the rest of 'us') have a message all their own. Surely the fact that those mysteries were never acknowledged by six years of teachers had to make us all wonder."

I wrote these words more than three decades ago in "A Personal Note" at the end of the first book I ever published. Titled *Like Me,* the book used photos and words (and a massive dose of idealism) to introduce young children to their retarded peers.

Quaint as it may seem today, *Like Me* was somewhat risky business back then. Retardation was one of those taboo topics, like sex, that we just didn't discuss openly... and certainly not at all with our kids. I guess we thought they wouldn't understand. Or maybe we just didn't want them to notice.

Turns out they did both. *Like Me,* in effect, gave young readers permission to talk candidly about retardation and invited them to ask questions and share impressions. They had lots of both as well as plenty of misunderstandings.

And you know what happened?

Candor happened. At least it happened on the part of the kids. And that made a lot of adults very uneasy.

Probably it's a different story today. Probably.

We produced our first brochure about a year after the Office of Special Education was born. It was a 12-page, magazine-style publication with full-color photographs of people—not products—occupying most of each page. Its primary purpose was to present the mission of Apple's new Office.

But when people reviewed it, that's not what they talked about first.

Similarly, with our first set of four black-and-white print advertisements. Each of the first three told a brief story about a disabled individual and accompanied the text with a handsome, professionally photographed portrait of that person. The fourth ad pictured those three individuals in a group pose with six additional disabled men and women. The headline of this last ad read, "Some people just don't know when to quit," and began:

> "When you're disabled, you have to be very
> determined not to do what people expect you to do.
> Which is very little.
>
> "Instead you have to demand more of yourself than
> you think you can accomplish. And then some."

In one of the ads, despite the fact that all were produced by Apple, no computer was even pictured. Just a portrait of a quadriplegic woman named Sue, whose brief story was headlined: "How to fight without using your arms and legs." Each of the other ads included an Apple computer, but the product was unplugged, the screen was blank and the person in the picture was using the computer as a chair.

The point of these ads was clearly not to tout the virtues of a personal computer, but rather the value of our personal relationships. First and foremost, they were demonstrating Apple's obvious intimacy with individuals like Sue and her counterparts.

But as was the case with our brochure, when people saw these ads, that's not what they talked about first.

Instead, in both cases, what we heard was how beautiful they were. How classy. How well written. How gorgeous the photography was. Almost all the comments were about aesthetics.

Which is precisely what we'd hoped would happen.

People would get to the substance of these materials eventually. We wanted them first to be impressed with the style. We wanted them to linger awhile with *the look*. And to come to see people with disabilities packaged in a way they'd never seen before.

This was, in fact, our mission. *What* we were about was *who* we were about. These people. These pictures.

Our emphasis on how they were portrayed may, in retrospect, have been a kind of bragging.

✳ ✳ ✳

In The Land of Disability, it's common for people to know more about an individual than to know the actual person. "That one over there has *[insert diagnostic label here]*." "She's the one who always needs help." "He can't hear all that well." "That little guy goes to a special school. **Nice kid.**"

A lot of this knowing about is made possible by a generally clever and safe use of words. The jargon and the rhetoric help us keep a comfortable distance from intimacy. And prevent us from having to display our awkwardness.

We don't like not being ourselves. And that happens a lot in DisabilityLand. We find ourselves off balance.

Visitors in this terrain don't generally have a lot of social practice with disabled individuals. They get good, instead, at pretend closeness. Too friendly. Too right-in-your-face. Laughing at the joke just a little too much.

And certainly relieved to have what was never really an interaction done with.

The marketing consultant was addressing a ballroom-full of people who'd gathered to explore matters related to de-institutionalization. One of these issues became particularly sticky: How much—if any—advance notice should be given to the neighbors about the four developmentally disabled adults who'd soon be moving into the large dwelling at the end of the block? After all, when a typical family moves into a new community, there's no preparation provided for the soon-to-be neighbors. People move. People meet. They become friends. Or they remain neighbors. Or not. Happens every day all around the world. Why should this move be so different?

But maybe it should be different if the new family isn't a "typical" family. If the new residence is going to be occupied by developmentally disabled adults and by trained supervisors who will also live there. Maybe there should be a meeting of the block just to give the neighbors a little information about the new residents and clear up any misconceptions people might have about developmental disabilities.

But such an approach has an intriguing irony when viewed by the people who already live on the block. "You're telling me," they might say, "that these people have lived much of their lives in institutions, but they're now somehow ready to live three doors down from my house? All four of them?"

Another might reasonably add, "Can I be assured that my children will be safe?"

And one more might say, "If having *those* people move into that residence is pretty much the same as having *any* new people move into that residence, then why did you feel the need to hold this meeting? We've never had this kind of meeting prior to anyone else moving in."

That, of course, is the irony: Everything will be more or less just the same but also pretty different. Understand?

It's an issue not easily resolved. More than one unoccupied home, in fact, has been mysteriously burned to the ground after a cordial get-together was organized to pre-introduce the new neighbors.

So what do you do?

I don't know, but I'll tell you what the marketing consultant (of all people) had to say on the subject. It was the most repugnant piece of advice I'd ever heard. But listen to it just the same.

"One way to think about ushering this new group of folks into the new community," he said, "is to consider that what you're really doing is *marketing defective merchandise.*"

(I warned you.)

The room was immediately uncomfortable.

Soon after, the reality underneath the repugnance started to make a strange kind of sense. And new strategies began to take shape.

✳ ✳ ✳

A blind student transferred into the sophomore class, which up to that point had been completely non-blind. My natural inclination was to be as helpful as possible. I was sure my classmates agreed.

So we read to him, when he asked. And we helped him find his way around the campus. We helped him with his homework, when he asked. And we accompanied him to the grocery store and to the Laundromat and to just about anywhere else he asked. The guy is disabled, for crying out loud. How can you stand by and not help?

We were feeling good about ourselves. And that feeling lasted about a week. Which is how long it took us to realize that this guy was a first-class jerk. But he was also still blind. How could we refuse his requests for assistance?

Because he had become the most demanding, ungrateful and un-fun guy you'd ever want to know. Blind or not, we just plain didn't like him. Talk about seeing the person beyond the disability.

That was a revelation to me. In the past, I figured that if someone has a disability, you should be nice to him; it's the thing to do. But now I was discovering that this guy with a disability was also a guy with a most off-putting approach to the world. I really didn't like him, even though he was blind. I wouldn't have liked him even if he were able to see.

To me, he had a far bigger problem than blindness.

✕ ✕ ✕

Our proposal to create a new division focusing on the needs of disabled kids and adults was approved. Exhilarating but not surprising. After all, how much sense does it make to ignore millions of potential customers?

I was called to the CEO's office the next day. "I'm not sure if you'll actually be able to make this thing happen," he said, "but if the idea looks like it's not going to succeed, you have to make me one promise."

I nodded.[1]

"You have to promise me," he continued, "that if this initiative is going to fail it will…" and then he said it:

FAIL HUGE

He could have said, "Be careful" He might have warned "Go slow."

Instead, the 2-word promise he asked me to make was to "Fail Huge."

Which is why we succeeded.

✕ ✕ ✕

1: Of course I nodded. I had a choice?

part III

LEAPS

"GENIUS IS AN AFRICAN WHO **DREAMS UP** SNOW."

VLADIMIR NABOKOV

It was mid-morning when I visited the Swedish school. Five or six doors opened off one corridor into different classrooms. One was for reading classes, another for arithmetic and yet another for arts and crafts activities. Everything looked neat and clean and colorful and typical.

And then I opened a door into a resource room for older retarded students. It was lighted only by red bulbs. A jukebox was playing. Several pairs of students were on a dance floor... dancing. Other students stood or sat by a bar drinking and chatting. A mirrored ball rotated slowly in the ceiling.

I was confused.

My hosts called the classroom *The Disco*. This was a real live classroom in disco-ness. Literally. And it was 11 o'clock in the morning in a resource room of a public school.

It seemed a little strange to me at first. But in the context of both the Scandinavian value system and the pervasive Scandinavian rhetoric, I was soon to discover that this classroom wasn't strange at all. It made perfect sense.

The Swedish people believe that school is a place that should help people— all people—fit into society. Not just to be out *with* society, but as much as possible, to be fully participating *in* it. One of the places in society where a retarded person is pretty likely to signal—through inappropriate behavior of one sort or another—that he does not fit in is a disco.

So why then shouldn't school be a place to learn disco-ness? How to ask someone to dance. And then to be able to dance. How to order a drink. And then to pay for it. And tip for it. How to initiate casual conversation. And then respond to it. How, simply, to relax.

In Sweden, very clearly, the rhetoric is all about mainstreaming. And when you listen to the Scandinavian people speak about mainstreaming and about normalization, what you hear are very pretty, very proud words.

But their sparkling rhetoric would have remained just that if classrooms like *The Disco* had not sprung from those words. In Sweden on that day, the rhetoric was both right and realized.

While education leaders, policy makers, researchers, economists, academicians, politicians and parents debate the great and complex and urgent questions that surround education today, it may make sense to pause, think about what we really mean by what we say and then ask, "What are *our* discos?"

✕ ✕ ✕

In the same Swedish school, in one corner of the gym, was a circular stairway that rose roughly 5 feet to nowhere. Some of the children I'd earlier seen at *The Disco* were lined up to climb it. It was part of their physical therapy routine, I was told.

But why a circular stairway? Why not a set of steps that simply go up one side of a big wooden block and then down the other? Why not steps, in other words, that look like steps one finds in the real world?

I suppose that depends on whose real world you're talking about.

"This is an exact replica of the stairs that some of our students will bump into when they begin taking public transportation on their own," the teacher explained. "Every bus has them. So rather than have my students be surprised by them, the gym is a place where they can practice. It doesn't take much."

A clever approach, to be sure, and one that came about for the same reason and from the same set of values that *The Disco* came about. The part of the explanation that remains equally impressive to me, however, was the end: "It doesn't take much."

✷ ✷ ✷

"NOTHING IS SO COMMONPLACE AS TO **WISH** TO BE REMARKABLE."

OLIVER WENDELL HOLMES

"I climb rocks smart," said Jake. "I read books stupid."

And just like that he summarized his life so far. He was better than any of his friends at challenges that were tough. It was "easy" that he couldn't handle. Easy like reading, writing and spelling. Easy like learning.

"While I'd be getting stuck, my friends would breeze right through. And when they went outside for recess, I'd have to stay inside to finish. I wasn't like them," Jake explained. "I was slow. Except on the rocks."

Jake continued, "But then I moved to a new school and I discovered two things that changed everything for me. First, I discovered that some of the other kids in the class had the same problem with words that I had. For the first time, I wasn't the only one struggling. Second, I discovered the computer.

"You know what the computer taught me? I'll bet you think reading, huh? Or writing? You'd be wrong. Even after just a few weeks, the computer taught me *confidence*. This time, in this school, with these kids and with this computer, I finally felt like I'd be able to breeze a little myself.

"Here's what else I learned. It makes no difference if it's reading or rock climbing. Once you have confidence, you're ok with the fact that sometimes you're going to have to ask for help from other people if you're going to make it.

"I wouldn't have admitted that a month ago."

✳ ✳ ✳

Apple Computer never knew about the Universal Access Society. It was not an official part of the company and showed up on nobody's organization chart. It had no manager. It was merely a voluntary group of a few engineers who decided to give themselves a name. It's what guerrillas do.

These were the engineers who developed the original accessibility software for the Macintosh. It was never a part of their (already overwhelming) jobs, so they worked at night and on weekends to make it happen.

But making it happen was not enough. Unless their work was officially a part of the operating system software for every Macintosh, it would do no good for anyone. And that's when the engineers demonstrated their true genius. And guerrilla-ness. When the company decided it was time to make some revisions to the operating system, the members of the Society simply inserted accessibility into the list of changes. They didn't ask permission. They went through no formal channels.

"It was the right thing to do," one of them said when the deed was done. "So we did it."

Another engineer added, "If we'd had to ask permission, someone might have said 'no.'"

They have never before been publicly acknowledged and their names will remain a secret. But because of what the Universal Access Society pioneered—and especially because of their "it's-right-so-we-did-it" mentality—the computer industry is now fully aware that some people aren't able to use a personal computer. They need, instead, a *personalized computer*.

✳ ✳ ✳

JUST ASKING.

You've heard it, too. "That person is confined to a wheelchair."

Does that make any sense to you?

If he or she is unable to move around without the use of a wheelchair, then what's confining about it? Isn't it, instead, liberating?

Confining, in fact, would be anything that's not the wheelchair. "That person," for example, "is confined to a couch."

But once he's back in the wheelchair, then he can go. He's unconfined.

If only it were just a matter of semantics.

Marcus was a young medical doctor from the Midwest. He wrote the letter to Apple on the morning of his 38th birthday—on the morning he learned that he had developed a condition called amyotrophic lateral sclerosis, more commonly known as Lou Gehrig's disease.

Because he was a doctor, he knew that this diagnosis meant three things:

1. He knew, first of all, that he was going to die.

2. He knew also that his death would likely involve a painful and progressive loss of physical functioning.

3. And he knew, finally, that he could never know how long his dying was going to take.

These are his words:

> "I'm writing because I need a little help. I've had my computer for several years now and I use it for almost everything. I use it to search through scientific databases. I use it to analyze my laboratory data. I use it to write my research papers. And when I'm not doing those things, I'm an adventure game fanatic.

> "From what the doctors have been able to determine so far, it looks like this disease of mine is going to be attacking my arms first of all. But I'll be damned if I'm going to give up being productive just because my fingers won't be able to roam across the keyboard anymore.

"So I'm writing to see if you can help me figure
out some kind of environment that will
anticipate as much as possible the course
of my disease... and that will enable me to
continue my work for as long as I'm alive.

"I've never been disabled before. I don't know
who else to ask."

Here was an individual who wasn't asking for sympathy or for charity. He knew
he didn't have time for such things. He was looking, instead, for "a little help" in
solving a very real, uniquely urgent and intensely personal problem.

We called him. And for about 45 minutes during our first conversation, we
began to explore all kinds of ways that we might design a productive future
for him.

While Dr. Marcus's letter was inspiring, it was maybe more importantly
instructional. It reminded us that what we were about was not technology. And
what we were about was not the *subject* of disabled individuals.

Rather, *what* we were about is *who* we were about: real flesh-and-blood
human beings. Individuals who happen to find themselves in particularly
challenging straits. And who, like Dr. Marcus, sometimes need "a little help."

Only a few months after we'd received his letter, Dr. Marcus was only able to
move one finger. He was writing to say he was continuing with his work.

✳ ✳ ✳

Today I searched the Internet for the phrase "leadership studies" and was almost instantly rewarded with a list of 121 million "finds." While such an incomprehensibly gigantic result isn't very useful, it does show that more than a few people have taken an academic interest in what it is that makes a leader a leader.

I, myself, have studied this particular subject not at all. I remain completely unencumbered by any objective data. But I have known more than a few spectacular teachers who seem to be natural leaders in their classrooms, in their staff meetings, in their parent meetings and in their lives. I doubt they've read the leadership literature either. They've been too busy leading. And, without knowing it, teaching me some lessons about leadership.

Here then, briefly described, are what I've come to understand as the five essential ingredients of leadership, as practiced by the very best educators I've known:

1. Vision

Every great leader has it. It's the ability to see around you what you, yourself, have never seen around you. It's what Jonathan Swift called "the art of seeing the invisible." It cannot be taught. It's magic. And like imagination, as Einstein observed, vision "… is more important than knowledge." It reminds you why you showed up and what you should be doing now that you're there. When great teachers look at their kids, they see them differently than others do.

2. Boldness

Great leaders never say anything non-bold. They never act in an un-bold-ish way. They talk loudly without raising their voice. They walk confidently without strutting. Their presence and their minds own whatever roomful of people they're in. Boldness assumes risk. It expects mistakes. It's not afraid to hit the ball. Boldness is not in the eye of the beholder but in the attitude of the leader.

3. Passion

You can't measure it, but you can always tell who has more of it than anyone else in the room. You can also tell how much it matters. The greatest special education teachers I have known are passionate not just about what goes on in their classroom; they're just as passionate about life itself. Passion is in their DNA. As George Balanchine said, "I don't want people who want to dance. I want people who *have* to dance." Passionate teachers *have* to teach.

4. Sense of Humor

When I think of the terrific teachers I have known, every one of them makes me laugh. Or at least chuckle. They take their pursuits seriously, but never themselves. I don't mean to suggest that they're either clowns or stand-up comedians. They're just amusing. They smile. George S. Merriam, who knows a little something about words, referred to sense of humor as "the oil of life's engine." Funny how critical it is. It's the lifeblood of the classroom teacher.

5. Accomplishment

You cannot get a high score on a multiple-choice test about creativity and then brag about how creative you are to anyone who'll listen. To be seen as creative, you have to "do" creative. To lead is to do, even if the doing consists of getting other people to do the doing. As one of the shrewdest leaders in the galaxy tells us: "Do or do not. There is no *try*." [13] Teachers do. All the time.

A final observation about classroom leadership. My list of five essential ingredients should perhaps be a list of six or 17. Who knows? But in the end, my list is unimportant. What will matter much more is the list you should now create for yourself.

13: Yoda, *The Empire Strikes Back*.

Saul Bellow described boredom as "the shriek of unused capacities." In the hospital, sick kids shriek a lot.

When the hospital staff was asked to help some young patients "blow up the boredom," they came up with the usual. Board games. Magazines. Writing. Arts and crafts. Decorations. Maybe a party. And so on.

Completely dissatisfied, the kids got online and asked for suggestions from others like themselves. The first two activities they received were:

> Activity One: Discover 10 new things you can do with hospital food (because you're not going to eat it anyway, are you?).

> Activity Two: Draw a map showing the fastest escape routes from your hospital room to any-where else in the world you'd rather be.

Many of the suggestions that followed can't be repeated here for reasons of propriety. It's fair to say, however, that they went well beyond anything that the hospital staff recommended.

None of them were boring.

And the list keeps growing.

✳ ✳ ✳

"THE CHILD MUST KNOW THAT HE IS **A MIRACLE;** THAT SINCE THE BEGINNING OF THE WORLD THERE HASN'T BEEN, AND UNTIL THE END OF THE WORLD THERE WILL NOT BE, ANOTHER CHILD LIKE HIM."

PABLO CASALS

The list of luminaries reported to have learning disabilities of one kind or another is impressive. A small sampling:

Albert Einstein, Galileo, Thomas Edison, Mozart,
General George Patton, Leonardo da Vinci,
F. Scott Fitzgerald, Eleanor Roosevelt, Walt Disney,
John Lennon, Louis Pasteur, George C. Scott,
James Earl Jones, Winston Churchill, Henry Ford,
Dwight D. Eisenhower, Jules Verne, Wendy Wasserstein,
George Bernard Shaw, Alexander Graham Bell,
Beethoven, Woodrow Wilson, Agatha Christie,
Magic Johnson and Hans Christian Andersen

Sam isn't on the list. He's only 15. But those who know him well figure it's just a matter of time before he joins the group.

"He's the last person you'd expect to launch a war *of* words," Sam's teacher explained. "His wars have always been *with* words. And in the past seven years, he's usually the one waving the white flag."

"I look foolish on paper," Sam said. "I know it. I'm a terrible writer. Always have been. Which is why I almost never write."

And then Sam spotted the five-legged frog and his new life as a writer took off.[14]

"Sam learned that the frogs in the pond were being born deformed because the chemicals coming from a nearby construction site were poisoning them," Sam's teacher explained. "That's when the cause and the letter-writing campaign began."

"They weren't complicated letters," Sam recalled. "More like notes in the beginning. But they did describe exactly what was happening in the pond. I wanted that construction company to stop poisoning the frogs."

"His letters were never answered," Sam's teacher explained. "Not the first. Not the tenth. Not the twenty-fifth. But Sam was determined. And he kept on writing. The same student who had butted heads with words for years was now writing letters on a weekly basis.

"After several more months with no response," she continued, "Sam ended his campaign. He'd written more than he'd ever written in his life, but none of his writing caused anything to change."

Well, not for the frogs anyway.

(POOF!)

✘ ✘ ✘

14: Yes, this sounds dangerously close to becoming a bad fairy tale. You almost expect the word "POOF!" to come next. But trust me, that's not where it's headed.

A wonderful poster was put out some years ago by the Spastics Society of Great Britain.[15] In it, a fourth- or fifth-grade child is sitting at a computer that he's operating with a head wand. He looks proud and serious. The monitor screen is covered with lines of text. Across the top of the poster a bold caption reads:

> "Just because I couldn't speak,
> they thought I had nothing to say."

Lots of nonvocal people have much to say and with access to a computer are, for the first time, being heard: across a room, over a phone, even on public assembly stages.

For anyone willing to listen, nonvocal individuals will give you an earful.

✳ ✳ ✳

15: This anachronistic name has been changed to Scope, an organization that states one of its primary goals as the "banishing of disablism" (http://www.scope.org.uk/home/mission.shtml).

"WE MATTER."

LEWIS THOMAS

Connor's father referred to himself as a *connoisseur of hope*. "It's part of who you become," he explained, "when you're the parent of a disabled child."

Connor has cerebral palsy. He doesn't speak very much or very clearly. But with the help of his computer, he was learning to communicate in his mainstreamed third-grade surroundings.

In a small group meeting, Connor's dad addressed other parents of children with various disabilities who had also been mainstreamed in public school. "I know I'm going to sound like a typical bragging parent," he said, "and I apologize for that. But maybe like some of you, after my son was born I really never believed I'd have the opportunity to be a typical bragging parent. Especially about school. So just this once..."

And away he bragged to the nods and smiles of the room. "...and just last week," he continued, "Connor was voted by his classmates to be an alternate on the student council." Bigger smiles.

As he reported on Connor's other successes at school, it became clear to everyone that none of what he was describing had anything to do with academics. They had to do, instead, with Connor's being a new kind of presence in the world. "Now that he can talk—his way—he thinks about himself differently. You can see it in his face."

Dad continued. "He's learning how to stand up for himself. And to fit in. But what I really wanted to brag about most of all is none of that. It's something much simpler. Something I'd seen in other kids that I'd never before seen in Connor." Dad paused. "Connor is now able to defy."

He eyed the faces around the room. They knew what he meant. Some kinds of achievement can't be measured on a standardized test.

* * *

JUST ASKING.

You're standing in front of two doors. One is marked "Special." The other, "Regular." You can only open one. Which one do you choose?

. . .

Isn't it time to do away with "special education"? And why not get rid of "regular education" as well? Aren't both designations at best anachronistic? Do you know any teacher who trained hard to become a regular education teacher? Don't all teachers aspire to offer phenomenal education?

. . .

The term "regular education" is nowhere in my dictionary. "Special education" is. Could it be that after all these years there really isn't any such thing as "regular education"?

Among all the words written about teaching, there are two statements that have stayed with me from the day I first read them. While not intended as such, they capture, in my opinion, the essence, the specialness of special education teaching.

You may not agree with my selections. But at the very least, perhaps they'll prompt you to find your own.

Emily Dickinson once criticized the dull performance of a classroom teacher this way:

"He has the facts but not the *phosphorescence of learning.*"

That's the singular and almost-impossible-to-describe quality that the very best teachers seem always to exhibit: *phosphorescence*. You glow and you keep on glowing. And if you don't have phosphorescence, no amount of in-service training is going to give it to you.

Then there's the definition of "teacher" offered by a Roman epic poet named Quintus Ennius:

"A teacher is one who *gently guides a wanderer on his way.*"

Different wanderers have different ways. The great special education teachers, the ones who seem born to the profession—the ones who can do a great 50 minutes if all they have for curricular materials are three acorns and a Styrofoam cup—know that. They're very much tuned into individual differences, individual needs, individual styles. Very little of what they do, as a result, is canned or inflexible. A lot of what they do is experimental. They're constantly trying things, exploring new ways for their wanderers.

Magic happens in their classrooms.

This will sound like a commercial for a computer. It isn't.

These are, instead, the comments of a 13-year-old, nonverbal boy named Adam.

"My computer has been the best thing that has ever happened to me in my life. Now people do not have to read my words; they can listen to me just like everyone else.

"When I talk in my dreams, I have a computer voice."

Maybe this should be a commercial about communication.

* * *

"THE GREAT PLEASURE **IN**

LIFE IS DOING WHAT PEOPLE

SAY YOU CANNOT DO."

WALTER BAGEHOT

Some years ago, I was invited to visit a community residence for developmentally disabled young adults in Denmark. While I was there, two statements were made to me that I've never forgotten, and which I've yet to hear anyone in DisabilityLand make in the United States.

After touring the public spaces of the residence, my host asked me if I'd like to go into some of the individuals' private rooms. I would. And further, if it would be ok, I'd like to shoot some videotape so that I can share my experience with colleagues back in the United States.

This will be no problem, the host told me. But you have to agree to let us video-tape you as well. Certainly, I answered, but why?

"The residents are out right now working at
their various jobs and you may not be here by
the time they return. Since we're showing you
something very personal to them, it only
makes sense that we show them something
very personal to you. Which is yourself, the one
we let peek into their lives.

"It's a simple matter of respect, don't you
think?"

Later that day, I asked my host about what the community residence program needs to do in order to get its funding renewed. I described how, in the States, the heads of programs such as these are required to keep detailed records and submit these data to external evaluators for careful scrutiny. That submission is then followed up by a second submission responding to the evaluators' additional questions. Is it pretty much the same procedure for you? I asked.

Not exactly, my host replied.

"We, of course have evaluators, too—officials who make sure that we're spending our funds appropriately and that the program is running smoothly. But instead of the forms, we provide the evaluators with lunch and dinner and then, the next morning, with breakfast."

I was noticeably confused.

We believe that words and numbers can only convey a tiny bit of how our program works, my host explained.

"To really know whether the program is
succeeding and to determine whether it ought
to receive funding for another year, you need
to be in the place. Feel it. Smell it. Listen to it.
Meet the residents. Meet the staff.

"Become a part of who we are. Live with us for
a weekend. Eat with us. Keep your eyes and
ears open.

"And by the time you're ready to leave, we
believe you'll know whether we're doing the
right thing.

"Makes perfect sense, don't you think?" [16]

✳ ✳ ✳

16: It should be noted that this attitude toward bureaucratic requirements is not original with the Danes. As Will Rogers observed much earlier: "In the early days of the Indian Territory, there were no such things as birth certificates. You being there was certificate enough."

I have a suggestion for you. It's the only one I'll offer in these pages. It's the one that has most dramatically changed my view of the people who live in DisabilityLand.

If you're scheduled to go to an upcoming conference on Education, Special Education or even Educational Technology, get out of it. Don't go. And if you're thinking about registering for one of these upcoming get-togethers, stop yourself before it's too late.

I understand that there's value to getting together with colleagues and experts from around the world. And certainly it's instructive to roam the miles of exhibit hall displays to see the newer versions of what you saw last year (and what you could just as easily have seen on the Internet). But those two or three days of conferencing will be much better spent if you follow my one suggestion:

Spend time with an artist. [17]

17: Preferably one who knows little or nothing about the kids or adults you work with every day.

It makes no difference whether the artist writes, paints, sings, dances, sculpts, makes movies or does magic tricks. It does make a difference, however, that the artist will not have been steeped in the same jargon, rhetoric, beliefs and experiences with which you've become all too familiar. Because that's the unique value that the artist will bring to your work. The artist will view what you do every day with very different eyes. The artist will talk about your students, using words you've never used. And most importantly, the artist will challenge your long-held assumptions about why and how you do the work you do.

Before I suggest why visiting with an artist may be the most valuable experience you can give yourself this year, read the following selection of quotes from different kinds of artists. Then read them once again, this time keeping in mind your own everyday routine, your own way of working, your own approach to the world:

"Nothing happens unless first a dream."
Carl Sandburg

"I dream my painting, and then I paint my dream."
Vincent van Gogh

"I dream for a living."
Steven Spielberg

"There is nothing like a dream to create the future."
Victor Hugo

"If you can dream it, you can do it."
Walt Disney

"I shut my eyes in order to see."
Paul Gauguin

"It may be those who do most, dream most."
Stephen Leacock

and, finally:

"The best way to make
your dreams come true is to wake up."
Paul Valéry

If these were people who just said pretty things about dreams, you could easily dismiss them. But these are accomplished people, artists who put their words into action for everyone to see.

And the work of each one begins with a dream. To the artist, dreams matter.

Whenever has dreaming mattered to educators?

So don't be a conference-goer. **Be a dreamer.** Because dreamers make dream-makers. And dream-making may just be the most "special" part of special education.

"Most people think of this as a computer," he said. "But not me. When I look at this machine, I see a hundred thousand paintbrushes and a million different colors. All at the tips of my fingers."

Realizing what he'd just said, he paused for a smile. Because of an accident suffered several years earlier, he had no fingertips that actually worked. So he operates his computer differently. He makes it work *his* way so that he can continue to grow his graphic design business.

"When I stop to think about what I've been able to accomplish since the accident," he says, "I find myself sitting up a little straighter in this wheelchair.

"Then I grab a new brush—any brush in the world—pick a new color—any color in the rainbow—and I'm back to work. If you had told me a couple of years ago that I'd be growing a successful business, I wouldn't have believed you. Nobody would.

"Yet here I am. With my brushes, my colors and the 12 people I've hired so far to help me out."

✻ ✻ ✻

We'll call him James. He was born into a household that was filled with music. His dad, especially, was a well-known jazz artist, and when he had time, he'd show James how to play. How to sing. How to write down whatever music was inside his head.

As James got older, there were those who said that James was getting to be a better jazz musician than his dad. He had a future in this business, they agreed.

When James turned 20, he was in a car accident that left him paralyzed from the neck down. So much for his future in jazz, they said.

At the Rehab Center, after they patched him up, they asked James, "What do you want to be now?"

"All I am is a jazz musician," he answered. "That's what I know. That's who I was. That's who I want to be."

"Probably not in the cards, anymore," they told him. "But let's try placing this thin brush between your teeth to see if you can learn to become a different kind of artist. A painter."

Ever the gentleman, James spit out the brush. "I write jazz. I play jazz. That's what I'm going to continue to do."

Fast-forward about a year. James was invited to deliver a speech at the Annual Conference of the American Occupational Therapy Association. He wheeled to the center of the stage and positioned himself in front of a Macintosh. He smiled. And with the help of his computer, some music software, a gadget that he wore on his head that allowed him to control the computer and an array of speakers, James began to play. It was an instrumental that he created just for this occasion. It was jazz. His jazz. And the place went wild. Hundreds of therapists swaying, bouncing, snapping fingers, tapping toes.

And it was good jazz. Not good jazz for a disabled guy, but just plain good jazz. He continued to smile, and with each round of applause he gave his audience a little more of what was inside his head.

To this day, James sends recordings of his music back to the Rehab Center that told him who he'd never be. He hopes they enjoy who he's become.

Again.

✳ ✳ ✳

His older daughter, Anne, is 12 and, in his words, a mile-a-minute non-stop talker. Jen, his younger daughter is 10, also an energetic communicator, but not with her voice. The few sounds she utters are used for emphasis and to convey emotion. "A non-verbal orator," her father calls her.

Two weeks ago, a Tango! entered their lives. Not the dance. The 6-button device. The Quick Start Guide to this stylish communication product begins as follows:

You're not going to believe this.

In just 30 minutes, you're going to feel comfortable using the most technologically advanced speech-generating device on the planet.

Hype? Hyperbole? An advertisement?

"The girls' bedrooms are across the hall from each other," Dad explained. "And last night for the first time in my life I found myself saying, 'OK, girls. Time to quiet down and go to sleep.'"

"As parental directives go, it's a classic right? It just wasn't ever a classic for me."

Dad continued. "Jen has been messing with the Tango! from the minute we took it out of the box. It's become her constant companion. And her voice.

"The girls continued to chat. I loved that they were listening to each other and not to me.

"Quiet down, girls," I repeated.

"Of course I hoped they'd keep on chatting all night long."

✳ ✳ ✳

We expect too much from personal computers. More than we should. But the hype is everywhere. And so believable.

It's especially everywhere and believable in special education.

Not that long ago, when computers first started showing up in classrooms, some manufacturers preyed on parental guilt to sell their machines. "Your child is going to school and he *doesn't* have a computer?"

The idea was that if the child had a computer, then this magical box would give him an edge…in everything. Name the subject and the computer would help the student do better. There's nothing it couldn't do. Without a magic pill to make you smarter, more athletic, better looking and instantly popular, the computer was the next best thing.

While we go on expecting too much from personal computers, we continue to expect too *little* from our special needs children. We underestimate how savvy they are, how capable. And they in turn become what we expect them to be: labeled children with predetermined limitations. Every parent has heard it: "Given her disability, you shouldn't hope for too much. She'll probably only get so far."

Years ago, many of us argued on ethical grounds against imposing limits on any child's potential. What can possibly be gained by stealing away hope and possibility from parents and teachers and siblings and neighbors? And by what right do you sentence potential in this way?

Today, we don't need to stand on shifting ethical sands to make the same case. We can instead say with complete certainty that because of what the computer makes possible, any limits imposed prematurely on a child today—any child—will be broken tomorrow.

That, in my opinion, is the computer's single most dramatic and pragmatic contribution to The Land of Disability. It disdains ceilings. It makes no assumptions about an individual's limitations. It cares not at all about a child's label.

Instead, like the very best special education teacher you've ever known, the computer simply allows for this: "Let's try. Let's see what we can do. And if what we try doesn't work, then let's try something else. And something else again."

Used skillfully and appropriately, the personal computer will always help any child bust through someone else's ceilings.

And that's how new futures will begin.

* * *

The Universe of DisabilityLand

In every part of the world, there is no end to the number of people, places, heroics, and absurdities that one inevitably will encounter in DisabilityLand. That's a good thing, I think, because stories matter uniquely. They humanize us. They provoke us. We remember them. We learn from them.

Stories are neither right nor wrong. They simply are.

Make of them what you will.

Too often, though, the terrific stories of what goes on in DisabilityLand go untold. What a waste. Especially because the stories of and around disability are usually written, compellingly, in italics,

Which is why SelectBooks has agreed to host a *DisabiltyLand* web forum where anyone can tell a story, share an anecdote or opinion or question. Or simply wonder out loud.

There are only 4 guidelines for telling your story on DisabilityLand:

Be brief.

Be appropriate

Be true

Be touched by what you write.

It's a simple matter to add your words to the DisabilityLand forum. Begin simply by going to: www.disabilityland.org. We'll take it from there.

Muriel Rukeyser, the highly acclaimed American poet and political activist, reminded us of the significance of stories. "The universe," she observed, "is made of stories, not atoms."

I invite you to expand the universe of DisabilityLand.

✳ ✳ ✳

"BE WHO YOU ARE

AND SAY WHAT YOU FEEL,

BECAUSE THOSE WHO MIND DON'T

MATTER AND THOSE WHO MATTER

DON'T MIND."

DR. SEUSS

Alan J. Brightman, Ph.D., has devoted his career to improving the quality of life of kids and adults with disabilities and to developing large-scale business opportunities to serve them.

Today, Brightman is a Senior Policy Director at Yahoo!, Inc. where he is responsible for making sure that all programs and activities across the Yahoo! network are accessible to every one of its more than 500 million monthly visitors, disabled and non-disabled alike. In addition, he is working with Yahoo! colleagues across the country to explore how the Internet can be used to change the tough, burdensome, confusing experience of being a seriously ill chid.

Prior to joining Apple, Brightman was the founder of Apple Computer's Worldwide Disability Solutions Group and served as its Director for 13 years. In this capacity, he was responsible for ensuring that all Apple products and programs were accessible to children and adults with special needs. In addition, he coauthored *Independence Day: Designing Computer Solutions for Individuals With Disability* and produced a variety of videos designed to illustrate the role of technology in increasing options and opportunities for all children and adults.

The work of Brightman's group at Apple, the first of its kind in the industry, has been widely recognized, honored and emulated around the globe.

Throughout his career, one of Brightman's principal aims has been to use mass media and mainstream technologies to substantially enhance the lives of underserved, often ignored, children and adults. He has published a number of books aimed at fostering fuller understanding and inclusion of stereotyped members of society. He also produced an award-winning children's television series for PBS as well as a one-person photographic exhibition designed to increase acceptance of disabled individuals. This exhibition toured the United States for three years.

Brightman has also served on the Board of Directors of the Starbright Foundation, an international organization chaired by Steven Spielberg that works to create new futures for seriously ill children. He was Executive Producer for Starbright of a series of programs—entitled *Videos With Attitude*—that go behind the scenes of childhood illness to illuminate the true, tough and occasionally humorous experiences of sickness and disability.

Brightman received a Ph.D. in Education from Harvard University and an Honorary Ph.D. in Science from The University of Massachusetts. He also received a Lifetime Achievement Award from Boston University.

✳ ✳ ✳

This book is beautifully decorated with artwork from NIAD (National Institute of Art and Disabilities), an innovative visual arts center assisting adults with developmental and other physical disabilities to find an outlet for their creative expression. Located just 6 miles north of Berkeley in Richmond, California, NIAD serves up to 50 adults from Contra Costa and Alameda County each day. Adults working at NIAD come from diverse cultural, ethnic and socio-economic backgrounds.

The NIAD program objectives are four-fold. It develops the capacity for creative expression in people with developmental and other physical disabilities, increasing their sense of personal identity and pride. It provides a gallery and other exhibition opportunities for their work, thereby validating their art, enhancing their self-esteem and providing them with earnings for their personal use. It fosters socialization and inclusion at the center and on field trips to museums, art galleries, artists' studios and community events. It increases the public's understanding of the artistic ability of people with disabilities.

NIAD was co-founded in 1982 by Elias Katz, Ph.D., clinical psychologist, and the late Florence Ludins-Katz, artist and educator, after ten years of pioneering work in the field. NIAD has received the Helen Crocker Award from the San Francisco Foundation, the Vineyards Award from the Golden Gate Chapter of the National Association of Fund-Raising Executives, and a citation from the California State Council on Developmental Disabilities and Advocacy, Inc.

NIAD is supported by the Regional Center of the East Bay, corporate, public and private foundations, individuals, NIAD art sales and special events. Even so, NIAD is constantly challenged to meet expenses, and we depend on community support.

www.niadart.org

* * *

Cover: **LISA BLEVENS**
Untitled 2
Colored Pencil and Graphite   12" x 18"
Lisa Blevens creates elegant drawings, paintings, prints and fabric art, all patterned with color in a myriad of small shapes-hearts, flowers, circles, triangles and stripes. Some of her art suggests radiating stars or suns, or features fanciful butterflies, pinwheels or clown faces. In some works the "negative" white space, defined on the paper by the dynamic outlines of surrounding patterns, comes to life and is essential to the composition. In another direction, Blevens often chooses to frame her painted quilting squares with black borders, offsetting and intensifying the colors they surround.

In January 1996 at age 28, Blevens wanted to take an art course and enrolled at NIAD two days a week. For the remaining three days, this petite woman stocks and bags groceries at a supermarket, a job she has held since 1986.

Blevens' art has appeared in several NIAD exhibits each year since 1997. Her work has also traveled to Santa Fe and Little Rock in 2000. NIAD's May 2005 exhibit, "Be Animated at NIAD!" featured two of her drawings.

Frontispiece: **SUSAN WISE**
Untitled
Ink & Watercolor   26" x 20"
Susan Wise has used her interest in crafts to develop as an artist in several mediums–quilting, basket weaving, painting, printmaking and ceramics. She especially enjoys making quilts, both patchwork and embroidered. She will embroider within an area to either accentuate or contrast the color and design. Her works have a tendency to reflect her fascination with animals.

Wise was institutionalized for a large part of her youth and became interested in crafts during her vocational training. She also enjoys caring for NIAD's garden, weeding and watering several hours each week.

Ms. Wise lives in a board-and-care home in Richmond and, over the course of the year, visits her family several times.

Acknowledgement: **SHANA HARPER**
Untitled
Linocut Print   37" x 12½"
Shana Harper came to NIAD in January 2005, shortly after her sister, Raven. In the short time she has spent at NIAD, Ms. Harper has been very productive producing jewelry, paintings, prints, and beautiful hand made scarves. Her two dimensional work has been highly influenced by Vincent Van Gogh and her choice of subject matter ranges from bucolic natural phenomenon to portraits and interior scenes.

Page xv: **MICHAEL SUTTON**
Untitled
Colored Pencil on Paper   26½" x 19¾"
Michael Sutton is legally blind but not to color. Whether in tempera, pastels or pencil, his circular, vertical and diagonal strokes lay on colors in clouds and sprays that light up the paper. He enjoys clay modeling even more so, since despite his poor vision, he can know through his hands the reality of the forms he wants to create.

He found similar satisfaction in a doll-making project in NIAD's textile arts class. Sutton described the doll he wanted to make to the instructor, who cut and sewed the fabric that Sutton selected. He stuffed the doll to give it form, named it "Teek Fatique" and invented a life story for it.

Sutton started working with art materials at age 39 when he enrolled at NIAD in 1989. His work has appeared in a number of NIAD exhibits.

He has a beautiful singing voice that lights up NIAD's weekly musical hour. Sutton is also highly articulate, and his creativity extends to inventing songs. Sutton lives in a nearby board and care home.

Page 1: **SYLVIA FRAGOSO**
Untitled (Angel)
Marker on Paper   10" x 8"
Sylvia Fragoso appeared on a Bay Area TV show in 1992 and was asked if she was a good artist. "I am. Yes, I am," she responded. As well she might. Ms. Fragoso's artwork has been exhibited in Miyazaki, Japan and Shanghai, China; at the Webb and Parsons Gallery in Vermont; Very Special Art Gallery in Palm Beach; Community College of Southern Nevada; in NIAD's traveling exhibit, The Creative Spirit; and at the Berlex Biosciences Corporate Offices in Richmond, CA.

Fragoso's art celebrates life in a playful way that reflects a love of nature, people, church, and the vibrant color combinations of her Hispanic heritage. In her art, she creates mosaic and web-like combinations in which people become animals, flowers become people, eyes become suns, suns become moons, and moons become faces and angels.

Fragoso was born with Down Syndrome in 1962 and started drawing and painting at the age of 22 after joining NIAD in 1984. She lives with her family in San Pablo and enjoys bowling and music. She has also participated in the state Olympics for gymnastics.

Ms. Fragoso's work was also featured in September 2004 at "Radiant Spaces: Private Domain," in Santa Monica and Irvine, as well as in a solo exhibit, "Expressions of Being Me," at Papillon Gourmet Coffees & Art Gallery in Lafayette, CA, and in the 2005 "Amazing World of NIAD Art Center" exhibit at the Concourse Gallery in San Francisco.

Page 17: RAY BROWN
Untitled
Watercolor on Paper   9" x 12"

Originally from Texas and born in 1957, Ray Brown is a relative newcomer to NIAD. Since arriving one year ago he has compiled a large body of work resulting from his very ambitious work habits. Ray doesn't waste too much time when he is at NIAD and when he's not making art he's proudly showing it off to visitors and staff.

Just like his work ethic, Ray Brown's artistic aspirations are not meager. He chooses to work in a variety of mediums including painting, drawing, and ceramics. His choice of subject matter varies depending on the medium, but overall Ray typically depicts birds, houses, and boats in a camouflaged field of intense color.

In addition to making art at NIAD Ray also enjoys being a mentor to some of the younger NIAD artists, making him a valuable asset in our creative community in addition to being a wonderful artist.

Page 21: LISA BLEVENS
Untitled 1
Colored Pencil and Graphite   9" x 12"

Page 24: BEVERLY "BUBBA" TRIEBER
X Man on Stool
Mixed Media on Paper   28" x 32"

When Beverly Trieber took up art at age 65, he made up for lost time quickly. Working with NIAD's staff he has created stunning abstract collages, prints and painted constructions made from all manner of found objects. Some of the materials he uses are scraps of printed fabric, yarn, textured paper, cardboard, magazines, newspaper pages, and other recyclables.

Trieber came to NIAD in 1986 after being institutionalized for developmental disabilities for most of his life. He now lives in a board and care home in Richmond and likes attending church and walking around town to chat with his friends, since he is especially sociable. He also enjoys a discussion or two about our current California Governor.

"Bubba" wears hats of various vintages and collects all manner of display and advertising buttons, which he pins in quantity to his clothing. The effect is rather like a walking collage.

Trieber's work has sold well to collectors, including Marwais Steel and Kaiser Permanente. His work has been shown in numerous exhibits both here and abroad and was recently exhibited in April 2005 at "The Amazing World of NIAD Art Center" in San Francisco's Concourse Gallery.

Page 36: VINCENT VILLANUEVA
Untitled (Cool Colors)
Mixed Media on Paper   24" x 20"

Vincent Villanueva's artistic style stems from his musical personality—he can be seen moving, swaying, and speaking in rhythm. His art is free, airy, and energetic with an emphasis on brush strokes that swing from side to side. His color palette varies from dark and moody grays, purples, and blacks to bright and colorful oranges and yellows. Whether Villanueva is creating a painting, weaving or print, his style always comes through.

Villanueva was born on May 18, 1942 in Texas. At the age of one, he moved to California. Villanueva has attended NIAD since 1998 and lives with his family.

Page 43: SHANA HARPER
The Maze Flower
Linocut Print   6¼" x 9"

Page 48: MICHAEL STAROSKY
Untitled (Smiling)
Mixed Media on Paper   15" x 20"

Michael Starosky first came to the NIAD Art Center in 2002 at the age of 48. He had previously expressed an interest in art but had never worked in any art medium with particular intensity.

It did not take Starosky long, however, to find his ability in verbal skills and poetry, drawing and illustration, and interesting and delightful work in clay. He is currently also working at print-making and his work is taking on a distinctive style of its own, characterized by a semi-realistic, rather humorous style which embodies his own quiet sense of humor.

Of all the artwork that he does at the NIAD Art Center, Michael says that he likes drawing in colors and working in clay the most. He has made many fascinating ceramic whales, which have shown both in the NIAD gift shop and in various exhibits. Starosky also depicts a recurring theme in his drawings, paintings and prints-the profile of a human head with an exaggerated nose, lips and chin.

When asked what he finds so interesting about the whales, he says, "I think they're neat!"

Page 83: HARRY INGRAM
Untitled (Two Sided)
Acrylic on paper   25" x 38"

For Harry Ingram, the arm and hand movement are very important elements to be captured in his paintings. He combines a myriad of broad and small brush strokes with his bold, explosive use of color. The strokes of paint swirl, curve, loop and fully cover the page in an overall consistent design of layered and overlapping patterns.

Sometimes Ingram integrates free-flowing alphabet letters, particularly the letters from his name "HARRY" among his random paint strokes. The "words" seem to take off into the wind of color.

Ingram was born on April 13, 1945 and is the second of five siblings. He has attended NIAD since 1984.

He lives with his parents in Richmond, CA and enjoys family vacations at Clear Lake, CA.

Page 89: SUSAN WISE
Untitled
Ink & Colored Pencil   26" x 18½"

Page 96: TAMARA SIMON
Untitled
Watercolor & Ink on Paper   23" x 17½"

Tamara Simon is an artist who shows innocence and passion in her art. Ms. Simon's portraits may at first seem naively rendered, but upon closer inspection, one can feel the spirit of her subject.

Simon's painting entitled "Home" was recently selected as one of four images reproduced as a card currently available at NIAD's gift store. She shows her home at night, filled with light and surrounded by stars.

Since coming to NIAD in 1993 at the age of 22, Simon has been painting, sculpting and making costumes and collages. Her work has appeared in numerous NIAD exhibits and at several Bay Area locations. Born and raised in the Richmond area, Simon lives with her parents and attends NIAD five days a week.

Page 112: SUSAN WISE
Trees Sunday Morning
Print   26 1/4" x 20"

Page 136: GAIL MOHR
Untitled
Mixed Media on Paper   16" x 13¼"

An exceptional sense of design and color are signature elements of Gail Mohr's carefully crafted art pieces. Specializing on small ceramics, Mohr's work on the wheel is precise and uniform. Her bowls are perfection and mirror those being sold in many retail stores.

Her carved ceramics are even more amazing. One tall vase shows a two-sided relief of scenes from Africa, while another ceramic of a cat morphed with a fish entitled "Cat-Fish" depicts precise imagery and Mohr's sense of humor.

Mohr was born in May 1959. She came to NIAD in 2003 after attending Diablo Valley College and now resides in her own home located in Martinez, CA.